When Loving You Is Wrong

You Is Wrong

But I Want to Be Right

GEORGE BLOOMER

D1113961

2 41.66
B655

Unless otherwise noted, Scripture quotations are taken from the *New King James Version* (NKJV), © 1979, 1980, 1982 by Thomas Nelson, Inc. Used by permission. All rights reserved.

Scripture quotations marked (NAS) are from the *New American Standard Bible*, © 1960, 1962, 1968, 1971, 1973, 1975, 1977 by The Lockman Foundation. Used by permission.

Scripture quotations marked (KJV) are taken from the *King James Version* of the Holy Bible.

WHEN LOVING YOU IS WRONG

George Bloomer
G. G. Bloomer Ministries
212 Corcoran Street
Durham, NC 27701

ISBN: 0-88368-504-3
Printed in the United States of America
Copyright © 1997 by Whitaker House

Whitaker House
30 Hunt Valley Circle
New Kensington, PA 15068

Library of Congress Cataloging-in-Publication Data

Bloomer, George G., 1963–
    When loving you is wrong / George G. Bloomer.
        p.   cm.
    ISBN 0-88368-504-3 (tradepbk. : alk. paper)
    1. Interpersonal relations—Religious aspects—Christianity. 2. Intimacy (Psychology)—Religious aspects—Christianity. 3. Love—Religious aspects—Christianity. I. Title.
BV4597.52.B57 1997
241'.66—dc21   97-24811

No part of this book may be reproduced or transmitted in any form or by any means, electronic or mechanical, including photocopying, recording, or by any information storage and retrieval system, without permission in writing from the publisher.

1 2 3 4 5 6 7 8 9 10 11 12 / 06 05 04 03 02 01 00 99 98 97

Contents

George Bloomer breathes a fresh wind of uniqueness into the increasingly popular subject of relationships with his latest release, *When Loving You Is Wrong, But I Want To Be Right*. By examining the very first relationships in the Garden of Eden, he speaks to the heart of every subsequent relationship, right up to the present time. This book is an enemy to mediocrity. Read it, apply it, and you will be too.

—Bishop Carlton D. Pearson
Higher Dimensions Family Church
Tulsa, Oklahoma

Foreword

*I*n *When Loving You Is Wrong,* Pastor George Bloomer exposes the Enemy's subtle relationship entrapments. Christians in increasing numbers are being drawn into these deceitful snares and away from the safety of God's provision. This exceptional work details the play-by-play tactics of the Devil to destroy our relationship and fellowship with God and others.

One of the strongest spirits that competes with the anointing in an individual's life is a soul tie, or soulish bonding. Soul ties strenuously wrestle in our minds for complete control and dominance of our every thought. With fleshly darts, the powers of compromise and logic strive to convince us that God will understand our involvement in forbidden relationships.

When Loving You Is Wrong is a vital book, especially for today when marriages are ending in a whirlwind and families are being destroyed because of one partner's desire for someone more enticing. We strongly recommend that every leader, whether spiritual or political, read this book to be enlightened about the plan and plot that is focused against us. Prepare yourself for a journey of revealed truths that have been manifested for this hour, in order for the church to be without spot or blemish when Christ returns for His bride.

Mack & Brenda Timberlake

Introduction

Recently, the church at large has been concentrating its message on prosperity and health—how to receive all that God has promised and how to maintain His good gifts to us. In some cases, however, when that focus has become distorted, it has spread spirits of greed, laziness, and selfishness through the church, while stirring up envy and strife. Yet, by themselves, health and prosperity—and even salvation—do us little good here on earth if removed from the context of relationships. Because God created us as relational beings, His intent in blessing us has always been that we share those blessings with others in order to strengthen our connections to other people and to Himself.

God has blessed me with the responsibility of delivering an essential message to the church concerning relationships, one of the most important areas of the natural lives of men and women throughout the world. I would like to share with you some of the many insights, revelations, and problem-solving truths He has caused me to recognize about this vital, but often little-understood, aspect of being human.

Through and after an intimate relationship, somewhere, at some time, each of us was conceived in the flesh, birthed into sin, and enabled to become the functioning males and females we are today. We are all involved in relationships with other people. Although the number of established connections varies from person to person, none of us are isolated hermits. In addition, individual relationships differ from one another in the degree of intimacy that has been developed. That level of familiarity can range from "just passing acquaintances" to "my one and only true love, my soul mate." Needless to say, acquaintanceships are much easier to make and maintain than are very close connections.

Throughout the world, most people at least acknowledge that a Supreme Being is the Maker of mankind. Almost all—saint and sinner alike—also admit that we need help and instruction in perfecting our personal, more intimate relationships. Where we seek that help, however, differentiates the saint from the sinner. This particular book is addressed to and written for the edification of the church: those redeemed men and women everywhere who not only recognize, but also reverence the holy God as the one and only Creator of mankind; who have acknowledged their sinfulness and have offered repentance to His Son, Jesus, the one and only Savior of men's souls; who know Jesus as their personal Savior and Redeemer, because He paid their sin-debt in full on the cross; and who, having given their hearts to God, also want to dedicate their minds and bodies, which are the vehicles for and the substance of their personal relationships.

Although the church is a spiritual entity, it is comprised of natural elements, flesh and blood, you and me, all trying to combine and unite together as the body of Christ. As flesh-and-blood human beings who are highly prone to error, we often operate our natural relationships through our carnal natures. Doing so can create unhappy and unsuccessful situations. Certainly, then, our God-ordained service to others is negatively affected.

While many Christians do abide in healthy, positive, productive relationships, many of us—perhaps too many of us—do not. As it now stands, members of the

10

church are spotted with the plague of forbidden relationships: those person-to-person, body-to-body, and soul-to-soul unions that are not sanctioned by God. Such unions are the intimate and potentially intimate relations between consenting adults that simply do not bear the Lord's seal of approval.

Forbidden relationships, to which an entire section of this book is devoted, are found everywhere in the unfruitful, unsaved lives of the majority of the earth's men and women. They should not, however, mark Christ's church. The evidence that they do is found in the abundance of problem-ridden unions, troubled marriages, and the open display of unconfessed sexual sins within the circles of God's people. By being able to know and recognize the symptoms and signposts of forbidden relationships in our midst, we can help prevent the sin and fatal consequences of individuals' unrighteous living from affecting and infecting the collective body of Christ.

If the truth were told, at one time or another in our lives, most of us have experienced the pain and suffering of at least one bad relationship. Notwithstanding, the liberating truth is that wholesome, strong, and fruitful unions can and will be ours when, by following the guidelines of the infallible Word of God, we learn to attract godly people into our lives. If you have not as yet learned the art of Almighty-approved attraction, you are probably making sinful strides in one of the following categories:

1. **Forbidden Relationships**: When loving you is wrong, but I don't want to be right.
2. **Fantasy Relationships**: When loving you is wrong, but I don't know that it's wrong, because I don't even know whether we are in a relationship or not.
3. **Fruitless Relationships**: When loving you is wrong, but I'm convinced that it's right.

4. **Faulty Relationships**: When the way I'm loving you is wrong, but I want to love you right.

If you find that your primary relationship does not belong to any of the first four groups, it must mean that it is a strong, stable one. You are the fortunate person who has been blessed with an alliance that fits into our last category:

5. **Fabulous Relationships:** When loving you is right, and all's right with the world.

Even if you are graced by God with such committed relationships, this book is still for you. Read on, and allow it to make you aware of the biblical origins of bad relationships, what God's Word says concerning these relationships, what it is that makes your own union successful, and how you can help others to be as blessed as you are.

I have chosen the title, *When Loving You Is Wrong,* with good reason. I needed to get your attention in order to deliver to the church this imperative message concerning forbidden, fruitless relationships. *"He who has an ear, let him hear what the Spirit says to the churches"* (Revelation 3:22). However, I did not want to leave you out on a limb somewhere, feeling guilty and condemned or hopeless and despairing because you have become enmeshed in an intimate relationship that is or has gone wrong. With the subtitle, *But I Want to Be Right,* I offer you the hope of restoration of right relationships by pointing you to *"the God of hope"* (Romans 15:13).

Throughout this book, I use the term *Mr. Goodbar* not in reference to the candy bar, as sweet as it may be, but as representative of the perfect, idealized mate or relationship. We do realize that God is the only perfect being and that our relationship with Him is to be the premier focus of our existence, and we know that we will not achieve perfection on earth in any relationship. However, this is no excuse for us to not strive for better, more harmonious relations with our fellowmen—and especially those fellowmen we call partner, spouse, mate, fiancé(e), and special friend.

In the natural world, the unregulated pursuit of the fantasy Mr. Goodbar image tends to blind the hearts and minds of desperate men and women, who are driven both by desire and enticement to seek the perfect mate in all the wrong ways, in all the wrong places, at any cost. When we do so, we always pay too high a price in broken hearts and unfulfillment.

If we follow God's prescription for relationships, however, our Mr. Goodbars need not be that expensive, leaving us in the spiritual, social, and emotional poorhouse. In fact, if we shop in the right places and select carefully, they can be most satisfying—and particularly sweet.

George G. Bloomer

Part 1

Forbidden Relationships

When Loving You Is Wrong, but I Don't Want to Be Right

Forbidden Relationships:

When Loving You Is Wrong, but I Don't Want to Be Right

B ecause the Lord has continued to open my eyes to the necessity of addressing the subject of relationships, He is constantly developing in me both spiritual revelations and an acute concern regarding this issue's relevance in the lives of His people. Thus, I cannot overemphasize to you, dear reader, the importance that you both be aware of and beware of forbidden relationships. Your favor and good standing with God depends on it!

God has forbidden His children to enter into several types of relationships. The following are some examples, starting with the most important:

³ You shall have no other gods before Me.
⁴ You shall not make for yourself a carved image,

or any likeness of anything that is in heaven above, or that is in the earth beneath, or that is in the water under the earth;
⁵ you shall not bow down to them nor serve them. For I, the LORD your God, am a jealous God.
(Exodus 20:3–5)

⁶ None of you shall approach anyone who is near of kin to him, to uncover his nakedness: I am the LORD. [A list of close relatives is then given.]
¹⁷ You shall not uncover the nakedness of a woman and her daughter, nor shall you take her son's daughter or her daughter's daughter, to uncover her nakedness. They are near of kin to her. It is wickedness.
¹⁸ Nor shall you take a woman as a rival to her sister, to uncover her nakedness while the other is alive.
¹⁹ Also you shall not approach a woman to uncover her nakedness as long as she is in her customary impurity.
²⁰ Moreover you shall not lie carnally with your neighbor's wife, to defile yourself with her.
²¹ And you shall not let any of your descendants pass through the fire to Molech, nor shall you profane the name of your God: I am the LORD.
²² You shall not lie with a male as with a woman. It is an abomination.
²³ Nor shall you mate with any animal, to defile yourself with it. Nor shall any woman stand before an animal to mate with it. It is perversion.
²⁴ Do not defile yourselves with any of these things; for by all these the nations are defiled, which I am casting out before you.   (Leviticus 18:6, 17–24)

³ For this is the will of God, your sanctification: that you should abstain from sexual immorality ["fornication" KJV].   (1 Thessalonians 4:3)

¹⁴ Do not be unequally yoked together with unbelievers. For what fellowship has righteousness with lawlessness? And what communion has light with darkness?   (2 Corinthians 6:14)

Because God prohibits such things as idolatry, fornication, homosexuality, adultery, incest, and bestiality, people often accuse Him of being mean and controlling, of not understanding the overwhelming urges of the human sex drive, and certainly of not wanting anyone to be fulfilled or to have any pleasure. They think God is cruel for designing humans with such powerful desires and then forbidding anyone to satisfy those desires except within the narrowly defined biblical constraints.

Even many Christians think God went too far when He declared close, *"yoked together"* relationships with unbelievers off-limits. Church pews seem to be increasingly occupied by lonely singles who, as they look within the sphere of the church for their lifetime companions, seem to have the same problem Adam did: *"But for Adam there was not found a helper suitable for him"* (Genesis 2:20 NAS). So, they want to compromise their Christian standards by expanding the circle of possibilities to include unbelievers. More than likely, the Enemy will have some good-looking, sweet-smelling, silver-tongued devil or vixen ready and willing to lure the believer into a forbidden relationship replete with sensual pleasures and lustful enticements.

At this point, duped believers distortedly reason that they had better marry their unbelieving companions rather than fall into sin and, further, that marrying them must be all right with God because the Bible says,

> [2] *Because of sexual immorality, let each man have his own wife, and let each woman have her own husband.*
> [9] *...For it is better to marry than to burn with passion.* (1 Corinthians 7:2, 9)

Yes, Scripture does declare that, but those words in the ninth verse are immediately preceded by this statement: *"But if they cannot exercise self-control, let them marry."* Moreover, the whole context of the passage shows that Paul was writing to Christians who may not have been gifted by God with celibacy, yet who wanted to live pure, godly lives. However, he still cautioned them not to go seeking mates, with the implication that they were to wait for the Lord to provide for their needs and to bring about any change in their marital status. He also clearly stated that they were free to marry whom they wished, but *"only in the Lord"* (v. 39). Thus, Christians need to exercise self-control at the outset of any encounter with an unbeliever. It is much easier not to take the first steps that might somehow lead to becoming unequally yoked together than it is to break the bonds that have formed once an intimate relationship has developed.

That still doesn't satisfy the heart that views God as harsh and judgmental in His prohibitions. Yet, as our loving heavenly Father, God wants only what is best for His children, and He knows that some situations lead to terrible heartache and ultimate disaster. Only because He wants to protect us from having to suffer the dire consequences of wrong relationships does He forbid certain alliances. By His merciful warning, God gives us the knowledge to avoid the Enemy's waiting trap, which is baited with the poison of the forbidden.

1

First the Bait, Then the Bite!

As we start to delve into this timely topic, let us take a look at the very first record the Bible gives of a relationship deemed unacceptable in the eyes of God. This first forbidden relationship took place thousands of years ago, yet it still has repercussions for us today.

> [1] *Now the serpent was more cunning than any beast of the field which the* LORD *God had made. And he said to the woman, "Has God indeed said, 'You shall not eat of every tree of the garden'?"*
> [2] *And the woman said to the serpent, "We may eat the fruit of the trees of the garden;*
> [3] *"but of the fruit of the tree which is in the midst of the garden, God has said, 'You shall not eat it, nor shall you touch it, lest you die.'"*
> [4] *Then the serpent said to the woman, "You will not surely die.*

⁵ "For God knows that in the day you eat of it your eyes will be opened, and you will be like God, knowing good and evil."
⁶ So when the woman saw that the tree was good for food, that it was pleasant to the eyes, and a tree desirable to make one wise, she took of its fruit and ate. She also gave to her husband with her, and he ate. (Genesis 3:1–6)

It is not coincidental that the first scriptural relationship of the forbidden type—that is, the type prohibited and disapproved of by God—is recorded in the Bible's first book. We also find in Genesis that the very first sin committed by humans was the one committed by Adam and Eve when they both ate of the forbidden fruit from the Tree of the Knowledge of Good and Evil. We all know this classic story in Scripture, many of us having learned it as children in Sunday school. But, when reading this passage, how often do we consider that Adam and Eve's sin of disobedience began sometime before Eve even took that first bitter bite and her husband, Adam, thoughtlessly followed her sinful lead?

In the first verse of the text, we read, *"And he* [the Serpent] *said to the woman,"* and in the second verse, *"And the woman said to the serpent."* Here in this verbal exchange, the discerning spiritual eye can see a catastrophe about to take place. Eve, the mother and symbol of humanity, had begun at this very point to enter into a definite, certain relationship with the Serpent. How? By merely conversing with him!

Through the bait of conversation, Satan convinced Eve to bite the forbidden fruit. Indeed, it was through the opening of Eve's mouth that mankind's initial sin was committed. However, I am convinced that the woman's fate was sealed more by the working of her tongue in unsanctioned conversation than by that of her teeth in the eating of unauthorized fruit! You see, long before Eve physically plucked the first pomegranate (or apple, if you prefer the common myth) from the forbidden tree, she had, figuratively speaking, tasted of Satan's fruit. And, unquestionably, Satan's fruit is evil.

We might even metaphorically say that Eve accepted and devoured a passion fruit from Satan because they had developed an intimate relationship. The Bible certainly alludes to this, but the actual level of intimacy between the woman and the Serpent is open to interpretation. Nevertheless, the important point for us is that they did have a relationship. Eve and the Serpent were involved, to whatever degree.

THE ALLURE OF SATAN'S SUBTLE CHARM

However, before we examine exactly how it was that the woman partook of Satan's evil passion fruit, let us first determine why it was that Eve even took a chance on exchanging pleasantries with the Devil in the first place. In the beginning of our text, we read, *"Now the serpent was more subtle than any beast of the field which the LORD God had made"* (Genesis 3:1 KJV). The word *subtle* is defined as "highly skillful or clever, cunning, deft or ingenious, not open or direct, crafty, sly, delicately suggestive, not easily detected, operating insidiously." Certainly, we Christians know Satan to be all of these things—skillfully clever, crafty, sly, insidious, hard to detect, and so on.

No doubt, on Satan's first day of business with this new creature, Man—and more precisely, Woman—he was surely on his best demonic behavior! With the very same tactics he employs today to tempt and trick God's people, the Enemy set out to ruin Eve. As a maneuvering serpent, he was slick, seductive, quick-witted, smooth-talking, cunning, quietly aggressive, and probably very good-looking. He embodied and offered to Eve, the original woman, all of the traits and characteristics women find attractive in men today. This silver-tongued Devil presented himself to Eve as a bold yet subtle rival to her husband, perhaps even acting in complete contrast to Adam in terms of his worldly knowledge, effervescent charm, wealth of compliments, and sophisticated dialogue. The Serpent was so successfully subtle that Eve failed to detect that he was a snake!

> [15] *This wisdom does not descend from above, but is earthly, sensual, demonic.* (James 3:15)

More than any of his outer charms, Satan used conversation as a weapon against Eve. He smooth-talked her into communicating with him, questioning God, overriding her husband's authority, influencing Adam to sin, and, ultimately, disobeying God.

> [5] *For God knows that in the day you eat of it your eyes will be opened, and you will be like God, knowing good and evil.* (Genesis 3:5)

INHERENT SUSCEPTIBILITY TO DESIGNER BAIT

However, as strong as the Serpent's nature was to deceive the woman, I am convinced that Eve's natural tendency to hear the Devil out was just as powerful. She viewed the Serpent more as a man than as a mere beast, because he differed from the other animals. The Serpent was a glorious creature with language skills and the ability to communicate, so Eve was naturally inclined to have a little talk with him.

One of my keen observances concerning the characteristic differences between the male and female genders is that, where men's attraction to women begins primarily with visual stimulation, women's attraction to men begins on the level of audibility. In other words, men see the physical appearance of women and are attracted by what they see, while women hear the voice and conversation of men and are attracted by what they hear. I have even gone so far as to coin the term *ear-voyancy* to describe women's supersensitivity to what they hear. In chapters to follow, this subject of women's ear-voyancy, as well as other issues related to the differences between males and females, will be further explored. Right now, however, it is crucial to the spiritual interpretation of the story of Eve and the Serpent that I point out that the Serpent was able to seduce the woman into sampling his own evil, poisonous, demonic passion fruit (which subsequently caused her to eat of the actual fruit forbidden by God), through the persuasive power of his tongue.

> [21] *Death and life are in the power of the tongue, and those who love it will eat its fruit.*
>
> (Proverbs 18:21)

> [8] *But no man can tame the tongue. It is an unruly evil, full of deadly poison.*　　　(James 3:8)

Satan, then, with all the selfish, ungodly motives of a homewrecker, took advantage of Eve's predisposed susceptibility to what is said, spoken, and audible, by which he lured her into being unfaithful to Adam and to God. He is very skilled at *"enticing unstable souls"* (2 Peter 2:14), employing whatever means will work on each person.

> [14] *And no wonder! For Satan himself transforms himself into an angel of light* [in this case, the Serpent].
> [15] *Therefore it is no great thing if his ministers also transform themselves into ministers of righteousness, whose end will be according to their works.*　　　(2 Corinthians 11:14–15)

Exploiting her vulnerability to what she heard, the Serpent used his tongue as a power tool against the woman to hammer at and sand down her natural and spiritual defenses—her faith in and her faithfulness to her husband and to God. By engaging Eve in a verbal give-and-take, in a conversation, the Serpent was able to implant in Eve the seeds of desire and enticement, which are the components of all temptation.

I believe this very first occurrence of verbal intercourse between Eve and the Devil developed over a period of time, just as most extramarital affairs do. Although we have no idea exactly what occurred except what we read in Genesis, the development of this relationship to such an intense level—given the final disastrous outcome—would probably have taken longer than the time required to speak the few biblically recorded lines of conversation. Before Eve actually ate from the forbidden tree in the Garden, the first woman was doomed because she took the bait of intimate conversation. Thus, women have subsequently been susceptible to being taken advantage of through verbal persuasion.

> [18] *For when they speak great swelling words of emptiness, they allure through the lusts of the flesh, through lewdness, the ones who have actually escaped from those who live in error.*
> [19] *While they promise them liberty, they themselves are slaves of corruption; for by whom a person is overcome, by him also he is brought into bondage.*
> (2 Peter 2:18–19)

Eve's vulnerability as a woman—the emotional, ear-voyant, impressionable vessel with a tendency to internalize what is given to her by a man—facilitated the breakdown of whatever initial reservations she had concerning Satan, this new "man" in her life. She thus became adulterously impregnated with his evil seed. And just as Satan, in his own tainted, unforgivable past, had arrogantly challenged Almighty God and was thrown out of heaven, so the seed that he was able to implant in the woman developed into a spirit called pride, presumption, or haughtiness. This vile spirit then caused her to usurp the marital and heavenly authorities in her life.

"SEEING" WITH HER EARS

> [6] *So when the woman saw that the tree was good for food, that it was pleasant to the eyes, and a tree desirable to make one wise, she took of its fruit and ate. She also gave to her husband with her, and he ate.* (Genesis 3:6)

If we take a close look at the above Scripture, we discover further proof of Eve's internalizing of Satan's poisonous seed, the words he spoke to her. While anyone with healthy vision could have looked upon the forbidden tree and, like Eve, could have seen that it was *"good for food"* and *"pleasant to the eyes,"* the Scripture tells us that the woman also saw that it was *"a tree desirable to make one wise."* But this could not have been visual knowledge; Eve could only have "seen" this existential quality of the tree—that it was desirable for making her wise—not by looking on its external properties, but by hearing, absorbing, and conceptualizing what the Serpent had spoken to her.

> [5] *Even so the tongue is a little member and boasts great things. See how great a forest a little fire kindles!*
> [6] *And the tongue is a fire, a world of iniquity. The tongue is so set among our members that it defiles the whole body, and sets on fire the course of nature; and it is set on fire by hell.* (James 3:5–6)

Clearly, when Eve ate the fruit of the Tree of the Knowledge of Good and Evil, having already mentally conceived desire by the implantation of Satan's deceptive seed in her mind, the particular piece of fruit that she chose was a bitter one, figuratively speaking. It was a selection that automatically contained the "knowledge of evil" and not a healthier choice, which would have produced a "knowledge of good." Not only this, but we also read that Eve convinced her husband, Adam, to likewise partake of what was evil and forbidden. How was this possible?

Because the woman had entered into a forbidden, adulterous relationship with the Serpent, she had become *"one flesh"* (Genesis 2:24) with him in a spiritual sense, as the intimately involved always do. She was so entangled that Satan's thoughts and spirit were now hers, and she hastily poisoned her husband with the evil infection Satan had given her, leading Adam to sin as well. Even so, in His later judgment of the conniving Serpent and the now sin-stained Adam and Eve, God severed with deliberation the unholy bond that bound Eve to Satan (in a later chapter, the issue of soul ties is further explored):

> ¹⁵ *And I will put enmity between you and the woman, and between your seed and her Seed; He shall bruise your head, and you shall bruise His heel.* (Genesis 3:15)

Furthermore, God reversed the curse on Eve from the satanic connection, by placing her under a lesser one:

> ¹⁶ *To the woman He said: "I will greatly multiply your sorrow and your conception; in pain you shall bring forth children; your desire shall be for your husband, and he shall rule over you."* (Genesis 3:16)

WHERE WAS ADAM?

Now, we cannot make a fair investigation of the story of The Fall without acknowledging the role Adam played in Eve's forbidden relationship with the Serpent. So the question we must address is, Where was Adam?

> ⁵ *And if a man also strive for masteries, yet is he not crowned, except he strive lawfully.*
> ⁶ *The husbandman that laboureth must be first partaker of the fruits.* (2 Timothy 2:5–6 KJV)

28

Adam, clearly, was not around—at least not mentally. He was nowhere to be found when Satan, this "new guy in town," was seducing his wife. He was somewhere else, concentrating on his own business, striving for mastery as *"the husbandman,"* planning and tending to the Garden, if only in his mind. Such is the way we know present-day men, possessors of that original Adamic nature, to be.

A DIFFERENCE IN PERSPECTIVE

Women are usually attending to multiple tasks and responsibilities at any given moment, their brains having been specially designed by God with this flexibility. In contrast, men, concerned with the physical elements of life, are usually narrowly focused, whether it be on business, their cars, their personal affairs, or even on what Nintendo game they are going to purchase next! In fact, if one were to view an earthly man in the spiritual realm, he would be seen with blinders on either side of his head, blocking his eyes from seeing in all but one direction—straight ahead.

Men are very goal-oriented; their measure of personal success and fulfillment is tied up in their individual achievements. Still, in singularly focusing their attention, they must be very careful concerning those things to which they are being inattentive. Depending on what his focus is and what is going temporarily unnoticed, man's narrow-minded tendencies can be either negative or positive—and, sometimes, both simultaneously.

Allow me to give you a personal example. After eight years of ministering, I was accused by my wife and family of having an affair. The "other woman" was sometimes dark, sometimes light; sometimes tall, sometimes short; sometimes a child, sometimes an adult; sometimes masculine, sometimes feminine; sometimes a service, sometimes a conference; sometimes a seminar, sometimes a revival; sometimes the Bible, sometimes a hymnal; sometimes a pulpit, sometimes a pew. You see, this affair of mine was not with a woman; it was with the church. I was giving her the best I had to offer—my time, attention, and care.

Like me, Adam was engrossed in what was his to do, but not with what was his—the woman. His preoccupation with the tasks God had given him to do made room for the Serpent to move in on what was Adam's territory—both in the sense of the physical area of the Garden and, clearly, in his relationship with Eve—and set up shop there. At the same time, Adam's inattentiveness was possibly enough motivation for Eve to be wanton and gave space for her to receive from the Serpent what she "couldn't get at home." And so, the first forbidden relationship was born.

A WORD TO THE WISE

In summary, it was in a forbidden relationship that the Serpent planted in Eve a corrupt seed of desire. The seed was watered by illicit conversation. He gained her confidence. She let her hair down. He moved into her emotional closet. Her inner conscience was seared. And then came the inevitable harvest—sin.

Women, do be careful of what you allow yourselves to hear. When necessary, put spiritual earplugs in your ears to block out the unwanted advances, flirtations, and enticements of the Devil!

Likewise, men, especially at crucial times, allow your focus and preoccupation to include the woman in your life. Since Eve, women have been designed by God to seek and be receptive to attention, affection, and a gentle touch. When they receive all of these on a regular and consistent basis, they are encouraged to do what they do best: nurture success, in both their lives and in yours. Communicate with them on a frequent basis as well, and keep the Enemy away from your natural and spiritual doors!

[7] If you do well, will you not be accepted? And if you do not do well, sin lies at the door. And its desire is for you, but you should rule over it.   (Genesis 4:7)

[7] Therefore submit to God. Resist the devil and he will flee from you.   (James 4:7)

To all of God's people everywhere, it is in the spirit of loving admonition that I advocate the use of the preventative medicine of God's Word for your lives. Take it in full, daily doses to ward off the spiritually incapacitating virus of forbidden relationships.

2

Location, Location, Location

The story of King David's greatest sin is also the Bible's classic tale of adultery. Concerning desire, lust, love, faithfulness, service, deceit, and murder, the soap-opera-styled love triangle of David, Bathsheba, and Uriah quite obviously fits into the category of forbidden relationships. All the same, we must be careful not to become too focused on what the obvious moral of any significant passage of Scripture is, this one included, to the point that we miss the hidden revelatory truths God desires us to see and learn. Underneath the obvious moral of this fascinating story lies a most profound principle to be discovered: a person's location in life often determines his position in life.

> [1] *It happened in the spring of the year, at the time when kings go out to battle, that David sent Joab and his servants with him, and all Israel; and they destroyed the people of Ammon and besieged Rabbah. But David remained at Jerusalem.*

² *Then it happened one evening that David arose from his bed and walked on the roof of the king's house. And from the roof he saw a woman bathing, and the woman was very beautiful to behold.*

³ *So David sent and inquired about the woman. And someone said, "Is this not Bathsheba, the daughter of Eliam, the wife of Uriah the Hittite?"*

⁴ *Then David sent messengers, and took her; and she came to him, and he lay with her, for she was cleansed from her impurity; and she returned to her house.*

⁵ *And the woman conceived; so she sent and told David, and said, "I am with child."*

⁶ *Then David sent to Joab, saying, "Send me Uriah the Hittite." And Joab sent Uriah to David.*

⁷ *When Uriah had come to him, David asked how Joab was doing, and how the people were doing, and how the war prospered.*

⁸ *And David said to Uriah, "Go down to your house and wash your feet." So Uriah departed from the king's house, and a gift of food from the king followed him.*

⁹ *But Uriah slept at the door of the king's house with all the servants of his lord, and did not go down to his house.*

¹⁰ *So when they told David, saying, "Uriah did not go down to his house," David said to Uriah, "Did you not come from a journey? Why did you not go down to your house?"*

¹¹ *And Uriah said to David, "The ark and Israel and Judah are dwelling in tents, and my lord Joab and the servants of my lord are encamped in the open fields. Shall I then go to my house to eat and drink, and to lie with my wife? As you live, and as your soul lives, I will not do this thing."*

¹² *Then David said to Uriah, "Wait here today also, and tomorrow I will let you depart." So Uriah remained in Jerusalem that day and the next.*

¹³ *Now when David called him, he ate and drank before him; and he made him drunk. And at evening he went out to lie on his bed with the servants of his lord, but he did not go down to his house.*

¹⁴ *In the morning it happened that David wrote a letter to Joab and sent it by the hand of Uriah.*
¹⁵ *And he wrote in the letter, saying, "Set Uriah in the forefront of the hottest battle, and retreat from him, that he may be struck down and die."*
¹⁶ *So it was, while Joab besieged the city, that he assigned Uriah to a place where he knew there were valiant men.*
¹⁷ *Then the men of the city came out and fought with Joab. And some of the people of the servants of David fell; and Uriah the Hittite died also.*
¹⁸ *Then Joab sent [a messenger] and told David all the things concerning the war.*
²² *So the messenger went, and came and told David all that Joab had sent by him.*
²³ *And the messenger said to David, "Surely the men prevailed against us and came out to us in the field; then we drove them back as far as the entrance of the gate.*
²⁴ *"The archers shot from the wall at your servants; and some of the king's servants are dead, and your servant Uriah the Hittite is dead also."*
²⁵ *Then David said to the messenger, "Thus you shall say to Joab: 'Do not let this thing displease you, for the sword devours one as well as another. Strengthen your attack against the city, and overthrow it.' So encourage him."*
²⁶ *When the wife of Uriah heard that Uriah her husband was dead, she mourned for her husband.*
²⁷ *And when her mourning was over, David sent and brought her to his house, and she became his wife and bore him a son. But the thing that David had done displeased the LORD.*
(2 Samuel 11:1–18, 22–27)

The first verse of the text reveals to us that Israel's greatest and most beloved leader, King David, was—as are all people at some time or another in their lives—out of position, because he was in the wrong place at the wrong time. How do we know this? The Scripture informs us that *"at the time when kings go out to battle...*

David remained at Jerusalem." In biblical times, during certain periods of the year, war would break out in the region. Such a season was apparently upon them. Presumably, everyone in the region knew this was the proper time for military operations; they had some sense of the biblical injunction that *"to everything there is a season, a time for every purpose under heaven...a time of war"* (Ecclesiastes 3:1, 8). So, all of the region's kings acted accordingly, fulfilling the expectation and requirement that they go off and sustain the regular protection of their territories through war. One king, however, stayed behind.

David himself was obviously very conscious of the season, for he sent Joab and his servants to the war on Israel's behalf. But somehow, David failed to look down at his own two feet and command them to carry him to the battlefield! Instead, according to this passage, he *"remained at Jerusalem."* He did not go when and where his kingly position dictated that he ought to go.

POSITION DETERMINES WELFARE

Your position in life means everything to your natural and spiritual well-being. By the word *position*, I mean "the point where you happen to be, naturally and spiritually, at a given time." I not am referring to your social standing or career status, even though they can be affected by where you are located at a given time.

Some of you reading this book happen to be out of position now because you were out of place in the past. For example, some of you are currently married to the wrong person simply because you were in the wrong neighborhood, the wrong city, or the wrong state at the time when you met. Possibly, you chose your mate because you thought he or she was "it" or simply because that person was the best of the group from whom you felt you had to choose. Still others of you are mismatched because you were mesmerized by a dance you had with the individual you are now with, while out at a party or a club years ago. But really, you had no business being at the club anyway, so you made yourself susceptible to the Enemy's tactics. With your guard down, you married that person, and it has been "hell on earth" ever since!

Thus, when living a life for God, position is crucial. Because David was initially out of his proper position, his actions became increasingly complicated, leading him further out of position to one fateful destination—disaster.

THE IMPORTANCE OF TIMING

Scripture tells us that David awoke from a late afternoon nap and walked out onto his rooftop. I imagine that because he was the king, David's palace sat higher than everyone else's, making it possible for him to overlook all of the surrounding buildings. So, he would frequently come out on his flat roof to survey the city. However, on this particular visit to the top of his palace, David paused for more than just a glance over the local region. He got an eyeful of a beautiful woman who just happened to be bathing on her rooftop at that moment.

Because David was not at war with the rest of the regional kings, because he was out of his designated position, the timing of his life was off. Every subsequent action he took was consequently not synchronized with God's time and place for him. David was out of step; his rhythm was off. Timing is everything, especially for God's people. It governs and determines the most effective moment for the occurrence of each event in our lives. Remember this:

> [1] *To everything there is a season, a time for every purpose under heaven:*
> [8] *A time to love, and a time to hate; a time of war, and a time of peace.* (Ecclesiastes 3:1, 8)

Likewise, many Scriptures assure us that God regulates, monitors, and actually determines the daily direction and the moment-by-moment advances of His people:

²³ *The steps of a good man are ordered by the* LORD, *and He delights in his way.* (Psalm 37:23)

²¹ *For the ways of man are before the eyes of the* LORD, *and He ponders all his paths.* (Proverbs 5:21)

⁶ *In all your ways acknowledge Him, and He shall direct your paths.* (Proverbs 3:6)

For David, this was the season to be at war. It was not the time for him to be on his rooftop. Because he was out of his right position and timing, David was vulnerable to the temptation to get out of God's place for him.

A VISION OF LOVELINESS

While on his rooftop, David spotted a lady who was taking a bath on the roof of her own house. In Israel in biblical days, the homes were constructed with flat roofs. Apparently, these were commonly used for bathing. Most plumbing needs in biblical times were handled outdoors, anyway. Perhaps, people bathing outdoors was not an uncommon sight for David to have seen from his rooftop. Quite possibly, this woman was taking her ritual cleansing *"from her impurity"* (v. 4). Whatever the case may have been, on this particular, misguided, fateful day when David was out of position and his timing was imperceptibly off, he looked upon an exceptionally notable specimen of womanhood. This bathing woman's most extraordinary quality was her remarkable beauty: *"and the woman was very beautiful to behold"* (2 Samuel 11:2).

Furthermore, we read that *"David sent and inquired about the woman"* (v. 3), as he was obviously taken with what he saw. Notice that the text does not even bother to tell us that David lusted after the woman. Just by knowing that David was a normal, healthy man, no stretch of the imagination is required in figuring out his feelings toward what he saw! As it happens, position became a crucial factor in this woman's fate, as well!

Seeing the woman and having his passions aroused as he did, David was then in position to greatly err. He should have immediately gone inside, shut his eyes, and asked God for strength to resist this temptation. He also could have taken Job's advice earlier:

> *¹ I have made a covenant with my eyes; why then should I look upon a young woman?*   (Job 31:1)

THE DOWNWARD SPIRAL

God allows us to be tempted so that we may freely choose righteousness and to strengthen our faith. But in opposition to the way many Christians tend to think, temptation rarely comes at us as an instant heaven versus hell option. When we are being tempted, a more apt description of the scenario is a step-by-step choice and consequence, choice and consequence, in which whatever it is that we opt to do—whether right or wrong—has its own *"just recompense of reward"* (Hebrews 2:2 KJV).

Scripture portrays a progressive path or a downward spiral in the process of temptation. Pivotal in the process is the decision each person makes concerning whether to entertain the wrongful desire or to ignore it. From then on, with each step taken on this path, it becomes more difficult to resist taking the next step toward destruction or to choose to turn around.

> *¹³ Let no one say when he is tempted, "I am tempted by God"; for God cannot be tempted by evil, nor does He Himself tempt anyone.*
> *¹⁴ But each one is tempted when he is drawn away by his own desires and enticed.*
> *¹⁵ Then, when desire has conceived, it gives birth to*

*sin; and sin, when it is full-grown, brings forth
death.* (James 1:13–15)

Instead of praying and submitting himself to God,
however, David did the thing that is natural for men to
do. He watched. He ogled. And, more than likely, he envisioned having sex with her. The more you view through
the eyes of lust, the more you are drawn to sin as it takes
control of your life. Such is the evil, hypnotic power re-
ferred to by this illustrative Scripture:

> [47] *And if your eye causes you to sin, pluck it out. It
> is better for you to enter the kingdom of God with
> one eye, rather than having two eyes, to be cast into
> hell fire.* (Mark 9:47)

VISUAL STIMULATION

As discussed in the previous chapter, men are visu-
ally oriented and stimulated. It began with Adam, it became the inheritance of David, and every man since has
had an "eye problem."

> [20] *Hell and Destruction are never full; so the eyes of
> man are never satisfied.* (Proverbs 27:20)

> [22] *The lamp of the body is the eye. If therefore your
> eye is good, your whole body will be full of light.*
> [23] *But if your eye is bad, your whole body will be
> full of darkness. If therefore the light that is in you
> is darkness, how great is that darkness!*
> (Matthew 6:22–23)

David's "vision" concerning the woman he saw was
evident from his inquiry about her. He was informed
that she was the daughter of Eliam, the wife of Uriah,
and her name was Bathsheba. However, I am led to believe that David already had some idea of who Bathsheba
was. His questioning was most likely a formality, a con-
firmation of what he already knew. You see, David, as

the blessed, favored, beloved king of Israel, had to have been involved with the people over whom he ruled and at least passingly familiar with the private lives of his captains and generals. He must have been, for these were the men to whom the king entrusted the successful strategizing of battles, which had previously won and would continue to win victories in war for Israel.

Based on the proximity of Uriah and Bathsheba's home to the palace, we can safely surmise that Uriah was one of David's higher ranking men and that David already had some familiarity with him. Only the homes of the nation's most important men, mostly military officials, were located near the king's palace. In order for David to view Bathsheba as he did, grasping the extent of her beauty, the rooftop of her home could not have been very far away from his, given that telescopes and binoculars had not yet been invented. So, since David knew Uriah, a significant man in his army, more than likely David also knew that this was Uriah's wife he had seen.

BATHSHEBA'S PROPER PLACE

When viewed through David's eyes in her rightful position, Bathsheba was the respectable, untouchable wife of one of his army officials. David knew God's prohibition of adultery very well. He declared, *"I delight to do Your will, O my God, and Your law is within my heart"* (Psalm 40:8). Thus, he was fully aware of the Commandments that said, *"You shall not commit adultery"* and *"You shall not covet your neighbor's wife"* (Deuteronomy 5:18, 21). Whenever David may have previously met Bathsheba, perhaps at the annual military balls or other social functions at court, he would only have perceived her position as Uriah's mate and would have treated her with the gentlemanly honor and respect her position as an officer's wife was due.

However, out of place, in the wrong location at the wrong time, Bathsheba was stripped of the covering of her spousal position. She simply became a naked woman to be desired in David's eyes. This was true to such an extent that, after David had viewed her outside of her proper position, the respectable, untouchable qualities that were hers as a married woman were no longer regarded by him.

MISUSE OF THE POSITION OF AUTHORITY

Once David had inquired after Bathsheba and had, through messengers, summoned her to the palace, one can just imagine what took place. The entire scenario of their meeting was one in which David's position, again, became most crucial to the happening of events. Unquestionably, his occupational position alone was enough to accomplish for David both the acquisition and the seduction of Bathsheba. He did not have to do anything! He did not have to invite her to visit the palace—he was the king. He did not have to offer her an explanation for wanting to see her, a married woman—he was the king. He did not even have to be good-looking—he was, quite simply, the king. My guess is that if she was in any way captivated by David, it was more by what he was, in his position as the king, than by who he was.

THE ATTRACTIVENESS OF ATTRACTION

It is equally believable, too, that Bathsheba was probably not attracted to David himself as much as she was attracted by his attraction to her. As it happens with a lot of young women, Bathsheba might not have really liked the king, but she liked the idea that he liked her. Being found desirable in a man's eyes is a great compliment to a woman, which reinforces her self-esteem. Almost universally, attraction to another is sparked when the relationship with that person enhances the individual's feeling of self-worth. To put it in personal terms, the better I feel about myself when I am with you, the more my attraction for you develops and grows.

When the king's summons to the palace arrived, Bathsheba had probably been feeling more than a little lonely and unloved. With all of Uriah's military duties away from home—and with his commanding, authoritarian personality to match, no doubt—who knows when Uriah had last really romanced his wife? How often had he told her that she was the most beautiful woman in the world, how much he loved and cherished her, and how he couldn't wait to get home from the battlefield to her loving embrace? With her self-esteem most likely in need of some extra bolstering, it is no wonder that Bathsheba was attracted to David and responded to his complimentary overtures.

THE ATTRACTION OF MATERIAL WEALTH

Moreover, Bathsheba must certainly have been attracted by what David had. Without any negativity or disdain, I offer the suggestion that women have, by nature, a strong need for economic security, and in this sense they are materialistic beings. The truth of the matter is that while men seek from women physical embrace, women seek from men physical things. However derogatory this may sound, it nevertheless is according to God's grand design. God intended that men not only emotionally support their women, but that they also provide material support for them as well.

> [8] *But if anyone does not provide for his own, and especially for those of his household, he has denied the faith and is worse than an unbeliever.*
> (1 Timothy 5:8)

Thus, it is not unreasonable for a woman to expect her husband to take care of her financially, even in today's economic climate. She, after all, is then responsible for seeing that, with his financial provision, everyone in the home is well fed and clothed, that the roof does not leak and the furnace is working, and that the poor in the neighborhood are helped, in addition to ensuring that the household will continue to run smoothly and be well supplied in the future. The picture of the virtuous wife in Proverbs 31:10–31 certainly describes her as being materialistic because her orientation is toward the tangible provisions for her home, but nowhere does it imply that she is greedy or lazy. God gave us this scriptural model of the ideal woman for us to know He designed women with this materialistic perspective to benefit all so that everyone's tangible needs are met and provided for.

So, when Bathsheba entered David's palace, she became instantly aware of the splendid provisions he could make for her. While Uriah, making a decent living in the king's army, had most likely provided a wonderful home for Bathsheba, his money and fineries were simply no match for David's wealth and luxury. Moreover, David's palace was sure to have had every modern-day convenience:

1. Air conditioning. Twenty-four hours a day, seven days a week, there were servants with fans in their hands, cooling the stifling-hot air before the king breathed it in.
2. A modern telecommunications system. According to Scripture, David had men lined up from his suite in the palace all the way to his generals' houses. All he had to do was speak a word of command, and the message would travel from man to man to man, down the line, so that the generals could receive their instructions within a few minutes.
3. A Rolex sundial. Enough said.

Not only did David have these, but I imagine that he also had a designer wardrobe, which no doubt included snakeskin and alligator sandals. More than likely, he had also set a romantic mood with the sensual ambiance of expensive chandeliers burning with scented candles.

With the money and mood thus set as they were, it is hardly believable that there could have been any turning back for Bathsheba, regardless of how much she might have loved Uriah. At this point, even if she had gone back to him in body, she could not have returned to him in spirit. Snatched from a world that was comfortable yet humble in comparison to the extravagant elegance of David's surroundings, Bathsheba was now out of position, it is probably safe to say, for good.

A DISASTROUS CHAIN REACTION

Knowing that Bathsheba was married—and to whom—did not prevent David, after inviting her to the palace, from having an illicit rendezvous with her. Just as Eve, after taking the bait of Satan's poisonous conversation, could not prohibit the conception giving birth to sin, so the lusts of David's flesh could not be contained. Again, being a natural man, he had watched. After seeing with his eyes and coveting in his heart, he took with his hands and flesh what the law of God commanded that he not even touch: the forbidden fruit that was another man's wife. With Bathsheba, then, David willingly entered into a forbidden relationship.

> [4] *And she came to him, and he lay with her, for she was cleansed from her impurity; and she returned to her house.*
> [5] *And the woman conceived; so she sent and told David, and said, "I am with child."*
> (2 Samuel 11:4–5)

With Bathsheba pregnant, David realized he was in a great deal of trouble. To cover his sin, protect his reputation, and possibly even salvage Bathsheba's dignity, he planned a cover-up that involved efforts to trick Uriah—now finally a concern of David's—into returning from the battlefront, sleeping with his wife, and if all went well, convincing Uriah that he had fathered the child

Bathsheba carried. But all did not go as planned, because of Uriah's great faithfulness. More faithful to his king and country than he was to his own sex drive, Uriah, when summoned from the battle by David and then made merry with plenty of food and too much to drink, refused the pleasure of sleeping with his wife while his fellowmen risked their lives at war.

> [4] *No one engaged in warfare entangles himself with the affairs of this life, that he may please him who enlisted him as a soldier.* (2 Timothy 2:4)

In fact, Uriah was the only member in this three-ring circus who remained in his proper place and position throughout. Even when David had him placed on the front line of the bloodiest battle to certainly die because Uriah's undying commitment had thwarted the king's perverse plan of deception, Uriah remained steadfast in his loyalty. He even unwittingly delivered the very letter that commanded his sentence. Up until the moment of his death, he was ever faithful and obedient to David. By respecting his king's position of authority, Uriah eternally maintained his own as a good soldier and dedicated servant.

WAY OUT OF LINE

Being out of proper position, David did what anyone who has ever fallen out of line inevitably does: he made bigger mistakes. His initial determination not to do what his position dictated he do—go to battle—led him to err more, by first watching Bathsheba and then falling for the temptation. Even after committing adultery, David proceeded further in iniquity when he had Bathsheba's husband killed. His was an initial wrong turn that snowballed into blatant, willful sin, the wages of which were extremely costly for David: the child he conceived with Bathsheba died in infancy, and his kingdom, in both his lifetime and in multiple generations to come, became irreparably divided. All of these consequences happened because the once great king of Israel could not keep his place.

FINDING YOUR PROPER PLACE

Where do you belong? Where is your proper location? Where do you fit in? What is your position in life? It is essential that you know.

To discover your position in life, you must first *"set your affection on things above, not on things on the earth"* (Colossians 3:2 KJV). Continually seek God's pleasure and will for your life. In so doing, you will allow His blessings to find you. Wherever the blessings of God overtake you is your proper place to be.

> [1] *Now it shall come to pass, if you diligently obey the voice of the LORD your God, to observe carefully all His commandments which I command you today, that the LORD your God will set you high above all nations of the earth.*
> [2] *And all these blessings shall come upon you and overtake you, because you obey the voice of the LORD your God:*
> [3] *Blessed shall you be in the city, and blessed shall you be in the country.*   (Deuteronomy 28:1–3)

At the same time, be conscious of your attitudes, viewpoints, and outlook on life, and be mindful of the choices you make. These all influence your ability to hold and maintain your proper position because they all have consequences, whether good or bad.

GET OUT OF THAT TOUGH SPOT

Finally, dear readers, know that a forbidden relationship is never the proper location for you. You must be fully certain that all of your relationships—whether in dating, marriage, church fellowship, or casual friendship—meet God's standards and carry His authorization and approval. Guard your choices in this most important matter, and confirm them with the Lord through constant prayer.

However, if you recognize that a relationship of yours is a forbidden one, seek the deliverance of God immediately and consistently until you are freed. In the end, you are responsible and will be held accountable for the securing of your life's proper position. It is a place that only you will ever be able to have and to hold perfectly.

3

"It Cost Me My Hair!"

When you stop and think, it seems rather strange that Samson would love *"strange women"* (1 Kings 11:1 KJV). After all, he was a Nazirite, an Israelite who took a vow of separation and self-imposed abstinence in order to consecrate himself for a special purpose. As it turned out, that special purpose always involved some specific task in the service of God that would benefit His people. Given Samson's sacred pledge, why was it that the three great female loves of his life—his Timnite wife, a Gazite harlot, and the infamous Delilah—were all Philistines, the Israelites' most notorious enemies and definitely on the taboo list? Precisely because they were forbidden!

Despite the special calling on his life, Samson, like many of us, seemed to gravitate toward what was no good for him. The things he could not have became more desirable because they were off-limits. Clearly, Samson's renowned physical strength had its counterpoint in moral weakness. Willfully, in full knowledge of his sacred covenant with God, Samson entered forbidden relationship after forbidden relationship with the pagan Philistine women. His vow and covenant, however, specified that Samson live a sanctified lifestyle, in which he would not cut his hair, drink strong drink, or touch anything considered unclean, including strange women:

> [2] *When either a man or woman consecrates an offering to take the vow of a Nazirite, to separate himself to the LORD,*
> [3] *he shall separate himself from wine and similar drink; he shall drink neither vinegar made from wine nor vinegar made from similar drink; neither shall he drink any grape juice, nor eat fresh grapes or raisins.*
> [4] *All the days of his separation he shall eat nothing that is produced by the grapevine, from seed to skin.*
> [5] *All the days of the vow of his separation no razor shall come upon his head; until the days are fulfilled for which he separated himself to the LORD, he shall be holy. Then he shall let the locks of the hair of his head grow.*
> [6] *All the days that he separates himself to the LORD he shall not go near a dead body.*
> [7] *He shall not make himself unclean even for his father or his mother, for his brother or his sister, when they die, because his separation to God is on his head.*
> [8] *All the days of his separation he shall be holy to the LORD.*
> [21] *This is the law of the Nazirite who vows to the LORD the offering for his separation, and besides that, whatever else his hand is able to provide; according to the vow which he takes, so he must do according to the law of his separation.*
> (Numbers 6:2–8, 21)

[1] *[Like]* king Solomon *[Samson]* loved many strange women...

50

² Of the nations concerning which the LORD *said unto the children of Israel, Ye shall not go in to them, neither shall they come in unto you: for surely they will turn away your heart after their gods.* (1 Kings 11:1–2 KJV)

Ultimately, by pursuing the unholy thing that he could not have, the world's strongest man lost the vehicle through which his holy empowerment was manifested—his hair!

⁴ Afterward it happened that he loved a woman in the Valley of Sorek, whose name was Delilah.

⁵ And the lords of the Philistines came up to her and said to her, "Entice him, and find out where his great strength lies, and by what means we may overpower him, that we may bind him to afflict him; and every one of us will give you eleven hundred pieces of silver."

⁶ So Delilah said to Samson, "Please tell me where your great strength lies, and with what you may be bound to afflict you."

⁷ And Samson said to her, "If they bind me with seven fresh bowstrings, not yet dried, then I shall become weak, and be like any other man."

⁸ So the lords of the Philistines brought up to her seven fresh bowstrings, not yet dried, and she bound him with them.

⁹ Now men were lying in wait, staying with her in the room. And she said to him, "The Philistines are upon you, Samson!" But he broke the bowstrings as a strand of yarn breaks when it touches fire. So the secret of his strength was not known.

¹⁰ Then Delilah said to Samson, "Look, you have mocked me and told me lies. Now, please tell me what you may be bound with."

¹¹ So he said to her, "If they bind me securely with new ropes that have never been used, then I shall become weak, and be like any other man."

¹² Therefore Delilah took new ropes and bound him with them, and said to him, "The Philistines are upon you, Samson!" And men were lying in wait, staying in the room. But he broke them off his arms like a thread.

[13] *Delilah said to Samson, "Until now you have mocked me and told me lies. Tell me what you may be bound with." And he said to her, "If you weave the seven locks of my head into the web of the loom";*

[14] *So she wove it tightly with the batten of the loom, and said to him, "The Philistines are upon you, Samson!" But he awoke from his sleep, and pulled out the batten and the web from the loom.*

[15] *Then she said to him, "How can you say, 'I love you,' when your heart is not with me? You have mocked me these three times, and have not told me where your great strength lies."*

[16] *And it came to pass, when she pestered him daily with her words and pressed him, so that his soul was vexed to death,*

[17] *that he told her all his heart, and said to her, "No razor has ever come upon my head, for I have been a Nazirite to God from my mother's womb. If I am shaven, then my strength will leave me, and I shall become weak, and be like any other man."*

[18] *When Delilah saw that he had told her all his heart, she sent and called for the lords of the Philistines, saying, "Come up once more, for he has told me all his heart." So the lords of the Philistines came up to her and brought the money in their hand.*

[19] *Then she lulled him to sleep on her knees, and called for a man and had him shave off the seven locks of his head. Then she began to torment him, and his strength left him.*

[20] *And she said, "The Philistines are upon you, Samson!" So he awoke from his sleep, and said, "I will go out as before, at other times, and shake myself free!" But he did not know that the LORD had departed from him.* (Judges 16:4–20)

The most commonly known relationship that Samson had with a Philistine woman is the one he shared with Delilah. This strange, foreign woman became the

channel through which the terrified Philistines ultimately sapped the very thing that caused them to trem-
ble and made Samson exceptional—his superhuman
strength.

Delilah, who was hardly as true to Samson as he was
to her, could be bought! Each of the Philistine lords offered her some three thousand dollars to discover and
reveal to them the sacred secret of Samson's strength.
Falling under her seductive control and, likewise, a victim of his own lusts, Samson could not perceive the me-
thodical efficiency by which this calculating woman went
about earning her weight in silver through betrayal.

THE SEDUCTIVE TRAP OF MANIPULATION

By using the feminine version of the manipulative
ploy, "If you love/want me, you'll do what I ask," Delilah
was able to insist that Samson tell her what she desired
to hear. She persuaded him to cross the point of no return, which was the breaking of his godly vow and covenant. Not only was Samson not permitted to cut his hair,
but he was not allowed to discuss it either. However, this
is exactly what Samson did. The pestering, vexing Delilah eventually pressed Samson into revealing to her that
the secret to his strength lay in his glorious, uncut hair.
Upon acquiring this knowledge, Delilah turned on Samson and had his head shaved, which allowed him to be
taken into captivity by the waiting Philistines.

All of a sudden, Samson was bound and could no
longer fight off his enemies. At this point, in fact, Samson could probably not have even shaken loose from his
friends! Taking a quick mental check, Samson must have
surely wondered why God had taken his strength from
him. And as quickly as he wondered, he knew: because
he had reneged on his vow to God. The covenant had been
broken, and his strength had been removed. Reluctantly
reaching toward the breeze he felt on the top of his now

bald head, Samson probably released a sad sigh as he expressed, "But it cost me my hair!"

In sharing first his flesh and then his secret with the Philistine woman, Samson severed his binding covenant with God and lost his strength. The revelatory fact, however, is that long before Samson uttered the sacred truth of his vow to Delilah, his real strength—his spiritual strength—had already begun to dwindle. His moral might had actually started to dissipate when he first began to sidestep the conditions of his vow. Samson's tampering with the covenant began with his initial attraction to Philistine women.

> [1] *Now Samson went down to Timnah, and saw a woman in Timnah of the daughters of the Philistines.*
> [2] *So he went up and told his father and mother, saying, "I have seen a woman in Timnah of the daughters of the Philistines; now therefore, get her for me as a wife."*
> [3] *Then his father and mother said to him, "Is there no woman among the daughters of your brethren, or among all my people, that you must go and get a wife from the uncircumcised Philistines?" And Samson said to his father, "Get her for me, for she pleases me well."* (Judges 14:1–3)

Samson's desire for the forbidden was not satisfied by marrying a Philistine. His intensifying interest in these prohibited women culminated in his attraction to Delilah, yet his escalating lust slowly but surely weakened his invisible strength of will, character, morality, virtue, discernment, and judgment.

THE HIGH COST OF ENTERTAINING THE FORBIDDEN

Eve, long before the actual partaking of forbidden fruit, was doomed when she first entertained the Devil's conversation. David, too, initially committed adultery in his mind by watching Bathsheba. Likewise, Samson's moral strength began to abate long before he actually revealed his secret to Delilah and subsequently lost his physical strength. For Samson, the real loss came when he broke his vow. The source of Samson's strength was not so much in his hair as it was in the power of the covenant that existed between him and God.

We are all walking in a unique covenant with God if we have accepted Jesus as our Lord and Savior. We must be sure, though, to walk honorably in our covenants. Realize that there is no relationship good enough to cause you to violate that covenant with God or to lose the strength that is found in keeping your vows to Him.

> [23] *That which has gone from your lips you shall keep and perform, for you voluntarily vowed to the LORD your God what you have promised with your mouth.* (Deuteronomy 23:23)

> [9] *Therefore keep the words of this covenant, and do them, that you may prosper in all that you do.* (Deuteronomy 29:9)

Samson paid a mighty price for his forbidden relationship with Delilah. With you, a forbidden relationship may have cost you little more than your hair. For many, however, the price has been paid in a broken heart, a shattered marriage, or even a ruined career. For some, a forbidden relationship may have cost only the shirt off their backs, while others paid the cost with their lives. Yet, all have had to pay the exorbitant price of losing fellowship with God. Thus, we can all share in the knowledge that any way you entertain them, forbidden relationships cost too much!

Part 2

Fantasy Relationships:

When Loving You Is Wrong, but I Don't Know That It's Wrong, Because I Don't Even Know If We Have a Relationship

Fantasy Relationships:

When Loving You Is Wrong, but I Don't Know That It's Wrong, Because I Don't Even Know If We Have a Relationship

Relationships that are not based in reality can be as unhealthy and dangerous as forbidden relationships. Especially for females, imagined love and self-created romance can lead to emotional ruin. On the other hand, men are often susceptible to manufacturing flawless female fantasy figures and then becoming overly attached to the distorted objects of their own making. Because of the depth and breadth of feelings wasted on what was thought to have existed, the unfortunate fantasizer can be robbed of the opportunity to ever experience genuine love and affection, due to a broken heart or an unobtainable, impossible dream.

When imagination runs amok and a fantasy goes too far, it can become an actual reality for the disillusioned creator of the image. The fantasizer then begins to modify the real world in order to fit the illusion. Mentally, events are changed, conversations are revised, mistakes are corrected, blunders are perfected, flaws are airbrushed, gestures are distorted, and intentions are altered to adapt to the imaginary scenario. Eventually, this perfect fantasy relationship becomes so much better than any conflicting, imperfect, natural union could ever be that the person begins to dwell in the realm of the imagination rather than flesh-and-blood reality.

At this point, it is safe to say that an addictive mental stronghold has been constructed and reinforced. In biblical times, strongholds were fortress-like buildings, usually located near the center hub of a fortified, walled city. Built of massive stone, strongholds provided further resistance to enemy attacks when the city walls had been destroyed.

Like those ancient inner-city fortifications, a mental stronghold is an inner structure or construct that has been erected at the core of a person's belief system. Fortified by repeated reactions to circumstances and to evil attacks from the Enemy, the stronghold can become extremely resistant to being torn down. Because it provides a false sense of security and distortedly supplies some need, the individual finds it very difficult to get rid of the entrenched mind-set, even though the person may know logically and spiritually it is wrong.

A fleeting thought can lead to idle daydreaming, which in turn can develop into distorted imaginations and finally to the formation of delusional strongholds. Such is the progression with fantasy relationships. Based not on God's truth, but on the deception of the Enemy, illusory associations can nevertheless form powerful connections in the mind of the creator even though they are not real. And, according to Scripture, they must be broken up and cast down. Thankfully, God has not only shown us how to do it, but He has also given us preventative measures to take as well:

> [3] *For though we walk in the flesh, we do not war according to the flesh.*
> [4] *For the weapons of our warfare are not carnal but mighty in God for pulling down strongholds,*
> [5] *casting down arguments* [*"imaginations"* KJV] *and every high thing that exalts itself against the knowledge of God, bringing every thought into captivity to the obedience of Christ.*
>
> (2 Corinthians 10:3–5)

When we learn to bring that first fleeting romantic thought *"into captivity to the obedience of Christ"* by praying and seeking the Lord's wisdom about it, we will develop discernment about what we are thinking. Not every thought that we have about the opposite sex or a particular member of it will head us in the wrong direction. However, the earlier we can check out our thoughts with the Lord, the easier it will be to dismiss them when they are not godly. Thus, we can break the destructive cycle at the introduction of the "harmless" thought, before our imaginations take over and strongholds are formed. The process is the same when tearing down strongholds that have become entrenched, although it is more difficult to accomplish because of their strength.

Learning how Christians can get caught in the cages of fantasy relationships is one of the best ways to avoid the same traps. And, knowing there is a way out if you have become ensnared will give you strength to tear down your strongholds of illusion and delusion. May God grant you the grace and wisdom never to settle for a shadow of a relationship when He will give you the real thing.

4

Building Castles in the Air

Often in instances of fantasized love, women's own emotionalism, vulnerability to conversation, and tendencies to be receptive to what comes from men—attention, affection, encouragement—make them susceptible to developing imaginary relationships. Although plenty of men in the world deliberately and knowingly lead women on, impressionable women frequently mistake gentlemen's courteous treatment of ladies in general as being signals of personal interest. Needing male attention, women who are lonely tend to latch on to any civility or act of good manners, take such behavior personally, and then mentally distort it all out of proportion. A woman's natural receptive tendency to internalize what she hears from a man and how she is approached by a man can lead to her daydreaming about him and embellishing on the events.

Spurred on by romance novels and popular love songs, with their tales of love at first sight and damsels being rescued by gallant knights, the longing of a woman for such adoration can grow to such an extent that her mind will fabricate a romantic relationship, which supplies these dynamics that are missing in her life.

> [6] *For of this sort are those who creep into house-holds and make captives of gullible women loaded down with sins, led away by various lusts.*
>
> (2 Timothy 3:6)

This is the unfortunate truth about April, the woman who describes in the following story how she created for herself a distorted reality of love.

SOMEDAY MY PRINCE WILL COME

My name is April. For some time I was involved in a great relationship, the type most people yearn to have once in their lifetime. Tom and I met very casually one Monday morning as we both tried to squeeze into the same crowded elevator of the office building where I worked. My career as a junior account executive (a glorified label for a marketing assistant) for the largest advertising agency in town was going nowhere fast—that is, until that fateful day when Tom came to work at the same firm.

Since we had already met, the boss asked me to introduce Tom to everyone and acquaint him with the general office procedures. In those couple of hours, Tom and I got to know each other much better than coworkers generally do in a year or two. His personality was so open and his demeanor was so genuinely caring that I told him about my frustrations with my job and the "good old boy" network. With overbearing, cavalier arrogance, the account executives—and especially my immediate boss—would repeatedly dismiss my ideas as being unimaginative or trite behind closed doors, but then they would plagiarize them with clients, claiming personal credit for my original concepts.

Tom was assigned to my design team, but it was obvious from the start that he was being groomed to take over the position of our accounts manager, who was in turn going to be bumped up the corporate ladder. Nevertheless, Tom was always forthright with our boss, attributing winning ideas to the originator even when he could have easily maintained they were his. At the time I failed to notice that he was impartial with his encouragement and acknowledgments of the efforts of everyone on the design team. All I could see was that Tom not only liked my work, but he had also graciously risen to my defense with the boss on more than one occasion. I felt protected and valued for the first time in years.

Within a few months, Tom was officially promoted to the position of account executive, thus becoming the director of our design team and my new boss. With this change in status and power, Tom's demeanor remained the same. He was always friendly, encouraging, and caring. He took into consideration our individual needs and circumstances, never demanding that we give up our personal lives for the sake of a project, but always eliciting from each of us the maximum of our potential.

In the atmosphere of Tom's support and reassurance, my once wounded ego began to heal and my sagging mood lifted. As I felt better about myself and my self-esteem grew, my creativity blossomed. My input on projects became more valuable, and clients started choosing my sales campaign ideas with regularity. I was flourishing personally and professionally, thanks to Tom.

Tom began to take me along to client meetings and business luncheons. A new side of me emerged in those situations. Normally rather shy in social settings, I began to be at ease with clients, conversing warmly and developing a rapport with them. In what is ordinarily a scary, cutthroat world in which everyone is out to undermine everybody else, Tom valued my growth and provided opportunities for my advancement.

However, what was more important to me was the exhilarating feeling I got every time Tom complimented my appearance or held the door open for me. Previously, I had thought that such courtesies were demeaning to women, but now his impeccable manners made me feel desirable as a woman.

Sporadically, Tom invited me to lunch to discuss a particular project we were working on. He also called me at home on rare occasions after work for the same reason. Of course, the personal side of our lives crept into the conversations we shared. We enjoyed each other's company and grew to be great friends. He became my wise counselor as well as my mentor.

As our relationship was becoming increasingly friendly, my feelings toward him were intensifying. At home in my apartment, I mulled over Tom's every comment, every kind gesture, every knowing look, and I smiled with the thought of it all. Each morning and evening, I thanked God for bringing Tom into my life and asked for His blessing on our friendship.

About now, some of you might be thinking to yourselves, "Oh, isn't that sweet? What a beautiful love story!" But, I am sorry to say, the story does not end here. In fact, it is only the beginning of a new chapter in my life, a chapter I had no intention of writing.

Because Tom had once left a message on my answering machine when I was out shopping, I began to stay at home in case he needed to reach me. I made up excuses not to go to dinner or the movies with my friends. I even stopped going to my church's midweek Bible studies, which I loved. I told myself that the current client's business was vital to our agency, that we were in a crucial stage of design development, and that it was essential for me to be available as much as possible—for the good of the company and my career, of course.

LIVING IN DREAMLAND

Home alone, I dreamed of what it would be like when Tom would finally reveal his attraction to me. The chemistry between us was so strong that I was convinced he experienced it, too. Because of his special care and kindness to me, I was sure the interest was definitely mutual.

Intimate conversations played over and over in my mind. His voice alone excited me. We talked about everything intensely. More than once, even though no one else could hear, I burst out laughing as I remembered one of his jokes! Our bond grew closer as we spoke from our hearts, sharing our secret dreams and desires. As we gave ourselves emotionally and mentally, I knew that this compassionate, gentle man had won a place in my heart. Increasingly, I found my world revolving around him.

As I listened to him, I envisioned that I was a pillow for Tom—someone to soothe him, someone to provide peace, someone for him just to lean on and rest. I liked taking on that role because I wanted to be his special confidante, the person he turned to as his only trusted intimate.

There were many reasons why I was falling in love with him. He was a man who was strong, powerful, and authoritative, but at the same time he was caring, gentle, and expressive. When others admired his charisma, I was able to stand back and smile because I knew him. He was my friend.

Many times I wondered what he saw in me. We were two different people with two totally different personalities. He was open; I was closed. He was boisterous; I was quiet. He was outgoing; I was reserved. A girlfriend of mine who knew him once told me that because of the type of man he was, he probably had hundreds on his list of friends and that she was sure I was at the bottom of the list. She added that if all of his friends were ever in a room together, I would probably be the least visible.

Still, our relationship had grown to the point where I felt safe to believe I was the sole object of his affection, his girl. However, I tended to forget that someone had already beaten me to the first-place position in his life—his wife. Yes, Tom was a married man.

I had met Tom's wife a few times at agency parties, but hidden hostility lurked behind my curious smile when we were introduced. She became my rival. I resented the fact that she was legally attached to him. I needed him, too! He made me feel good about myself; he made me laugh; he cared about me, and I about him. I hated the fact that whenever she was present, Tom quickly shoved me backstage, yet when the curtain reopened, I was expected to do my song-and-dance routine as usual. Eventually, I could not play the understudy anymore. I was hurting and was tired of being the supporting actress; I wanted the leading role!

GETTING THE SHOCK OF MY LIFE

This predicament led to the only argument that Tom and I ever had. He had arranged a dinner party at a posh restaurant to entertain a potential client and help secure the account for our firm. Tom wanted the entire creative team to be there, with spouses or suitable dates. Since I had previously withdrawn from the dating scene, Tom suggested that I be escorted by a recently divorced member of the client's staff. Of course, I knew that Tom's wife would accompany him, and I was not sure that I could handle seeing them together.

Despite my inner conflict, I accepted the invitation. I was nervous, my palms were slightly damp, and my smile was completely phony. I did not want to say or do the wrong thing in her presence. Throughout the evening, I wondered what she was thinking about me. Did she see that I was too closely attached to her husband? Could she tell that I loved Tom? I tried to act nonchalant and show an interest in my escort, but I knew I was doing a poor job of covering up my real feelings.

As I covertly studied the way Tom was so solicitous of his wife, my great friendship with him seemed to collapse right in front of my eyes. Everything I had worked so hard to build was crumbling, and I had become unimportant. The curtain had been drawn on me, the leading actress was onstage, and I had to fade into the background and wait my turn again. But I had reached the end of my rope! I refused to play second fiddle anymore.

At that moment, I hated him for putting me in a position where I had to compete for his attention and love. Why couldn't we talk like we used to? Why had I suddenly become invisible? Was I simply a thing of convenience for him? I was so angry that I was about ready to explode. If it meant losing my special friend, I would be devastated, but so be it!

The night finally ended with Tom and I creating a scene—we got in a quarrel over the waiter's tip! Can you believe that? It was unbelievably silly. And it had absolutely nothing to do with the waiter; it was all about us. I do not remember all the details of what happened, but I know that I insisted and he insisted; I argued and he argued back, both mad as hornets! The debate ended with my not so politely storming out of the restaurant, leaving a perplexed Tom to smooth things over with the client.

The following day was Sunday, and I followed my regular Sunday routine, but my heart was heavy. I barely heard a word of the sermon because, throughout the day, I kept questioning myself: "How could I have been so stupid? What had I expected to happen, anyway? I knew all along he was married!"

I went through the motions of the day in silence. No one noticed my pain. I felt so used, so betrayed, so overwhelmed. My only release was in the form of warm, silent tears.

I took a personal leave from work so I would not have to face Tom. A week or so later, he called to see if I was all right, but he really wanted to talk about what had happened that night. When I finally admitted how I felt about him and that I was threatened by his wife's presence, he apologized for ever having done anything to give me the impression that he was attracted to me in a romantic way. He let me know that he was totally in love with his wife, his commitment to her was sacred, and he would never violate her trust in him.

At that moment, I felt as if Tom had suddenly slapped me. However, the shock of his words forced me out of my delusion and brought me back to reality. My mind slowly grasped the truth that our romance existed only in my imagination.

RETURNING TO EARTH

As a result of this fantasy, I have been on an emotional roller coaster, I have faced many days with uneasiness, and I have endured endless self-interrogation in a quest for personal authenticity. How could I have spent countless hours talking with him and being treated like a queen, a priceless jewel, a precious gem, and not indulge in that relationship all the more? It was impossible!

Yet, I had to admit I had deceived myself. Tom had never misrepresented his intentions toward me or singled me out for any special treatment. He had always been a gentleman and had never given me any indication that he was interested in me in an intimate sense. Out of loneliness, perhaps, I had misread his actions and had just let my imagination run wild.

Now, I had to deal with the reality of the situation. This man was simply not mine to love. He belonged to someone else, and I had to accept that fact. Deep down, I knew that God would never have blessed our relationship because He never endorses sin.

I have come to the place of repentance for desiring something outside of God's will and for not trusting God to supply all my needs, including romance and genuine love. I am learning daily to focus on the truth of God's Word and to capture every thought and bring it to Christ before my imagination gets me into another awkward, painful situation.

FLESH, LIES, AND THE DEVIL

We could engage in a heated debate over the origins of fantasies such as these that have become strongholds. Some people emphatically declare that Satan is the original source, since *"he is a liar and the father of it"* (John 8:44), and since he desires *"to deceive, if possible, even the elect"* (Matthew 24:24). Others insist just as strongly that our own carnal nature gets us in this trouble. They cite that in our *"flesh nothing good dwells"* (Romans 7:18), that man's *"heart is deceitful above all things, and desperately wicked"* (Jeremiah 17:9), and that as a man *"thinks in his heart, so is he"* (Proverbs 23:7).

I believe that strongholds are erected in our minds by the combined efforts of Satan and our own carnality. The Devil tempts us where we are most vulnerable, and our *"flesh with its passions and desires"* (Galatians 5:24) latches on, if only in the recesses of the mind. As this process is repeated, a mental structure eventually takes shape and is reinforced, becoming a haven in which to hide our pet delusions and distorted thought patterns.

However, if we are truly born again, we are no longer just passive spectators in these circumstances, simply reacting to Satan's lures. We have a choice in the matter as to who is going to control our lives and how we are going to live.

> [5] *For those who live according to the flesh set their minds on the things of the flesh, but those who live according to the Spirit, the things of the Spirit.*
> [6] *For to be carnally minded is death, but to be spiritually minded is life and peace.*
> [7] *Because the carnal mind is enmity against God; for it is not subject to the law of God, nor indeed can be.* (Romans 8:5–7)

Do remember that it is quite possible to be a Christian and still be carnally minded, *"indulging the desires of the flesh and of the mind"* (Ephesians 2:3 NAS). Paul wrote to the early church at Corinth, *"I, brethren, could not speak to you as to spiritual people but as to carnal, as to babes in Christ...for you are still carnal"* (1 Corinthians 3:1, 3). However, those words are in the middle of a passage on gaining spiritual discernment and wisdom and instructions for laying the proper foundations for living and building holy temples of God. In other words, Christians are to grow up spiritually and become mature enough to make choices through the all-wise inspiration of the Holy Spirit and not with their ignorant flesh.

> [14] *But put on the Lord Jesus Christ, and make no provision for the flesh, to fulfill its lusts.* (Romans 13:14)

> [2] *Set your mind on things above, not on things on the earth.*
> [3] *For you died, and your life is hidden with Christ in God.* (Colossians 3:2–3)

Our loving heavenly Father has not left us to refocus our minds on our own. Since our lives are hidden in Him, we can choose to respond to His voice and to walk in His vision for our lives. The Lord wants us to be involved in the most fulfilling, intimate, exciting relationships possible—first, with Him, and then, with the person of His choosing.

5

Ladies' Man Lost

When men are immature, impractical, or psychologically imbalanced, they are just as susceptible as women are to "living the lie" that imagination tells. And the fact is that men who name the name of Christ are not always exceptions to this tragedy.

In deciphering the different mental, psychological, and sensual tendencies of the sexes, I have observed that where women are primarily moved by what they hear, men are mostly affected by what they see, as I have previously stated. The visual information a man receives is what motivates, inspires, stimulates, and arouses him, especially where it relates to the opposite sex.

[20] *The eyes of man are never satisfied.*
(Proverbs 27:20)

[28] *But I say to you that whoever looks at a woman to lust for her has already committed adultery with her in his heart.* (Matthew 5:28)

With the certain understanding that men are primarily visual creatures, then, it is easy to pinpoint the origins and substance of their flights of fancy about females. Quite often, men's fantasies are based on those superficial standards established by sight.

ONLY SKIN-DEEP BEAUTY

While "Ms. Right" for the average man is usually a composite of select traits in a number of areas—including spirituality, personality, disposition, background, and interests, as well as physical appearance—for the fantasy creator the perfect woman's only substance is her physical aesthetic. She is an unrealistic creature of his imagination, a self-designed goddess whose existence and availability is never likely to extend beyond the confines of the creator's mind. This ideal female may be based upon a teacher or an older woman who impressed the man in his youth; a celebrity or fashion model who has been awarded godlike or sex-symbol status by the media; some other isolated, far-removed woman who is generally unobtainable by the man, such as an attractive lady he has met in the work arena; or a two-dimensional image, airbrushed to perfection, presented to him through the perverted realms of pornography.

Secular psychologists and therapists generally encourage the regular practice of daydreaming and fantasizing, telling us that having a "healthy imagination" is, in fact, healthy. However, where the Christian man is concerned, an overdeveloped habit or tendency to create mental realities is nothing less than futile imagination. The Word of God clearly speaks against this practice, because it is often a hindrance to the believer's spiritual growth and can open the door to perversion.

> [21] *Although they knew God, they did not glorify Him as God, nor were thankful, but became futile in their thoughts [*"vain in their imaginations"* KJV], and their foolish hearts were darkened.*

[24] *Therefore God also gave them up to uncleanness, in the lusts of their hearts, to dishonor their bodies among themselves.*

[26] *For this reason God gave them up to vile passions. For even their women exchanged the natural use for what is against nature.*

[27] *Likewise also the men, leaving the natural use of the woman, burned in their lust...committing what is shameful, and receiving in themselves the penalty of their error which was due.*

(Romans 1:21, 24, 26–27)

THE MACHO SELF-IMAGE

A popular truism within the circles of human psychology is that when a man follows after the unrealistic feminine images of his mind and exclusively seeks women of physical perfection for companionship, it frequently is a sign that he feels severely inadequate in some aspect of his manhood. A preoccupation with the superficial—those temporal elements of outward appearance that are subject to change with time and have little to do with the establishment of long-term, successful relationships—also suggests a fear of intimacy, sexual and personal insecurity, and a certain lack of self-esteem.

Another explanation is that the man who follows his fantasies may be an extremely high-minded, arrogant individual. In either case, these men distortedly believe that they are all the more manly when they have acquired or are accompanied by a certain type of female. The man who must have a "trophy woman" draped on his arm needs her in order to feel he can successfully compete with his male peers. He may use his female companion to provoke other men's jealousy of him for his capturing such a great-looking "prize."

Nevertheless, such is a most unhealthy and ungodly mentality, a perverse way of viewing women. This behavior, which is the result of a stronghold having been allowed to develop, must be cast down—and cast out—especially from the church, since it does not suit the man who professes salvation.

> [4] *For the weapons of our warfare are not carnal but mighty in God for pulling down strongholds,*
> [5] *casting down arguments ["imaginations" KJV] and every high thing that exalts itself against the knowledge of God, bringing every thought into captivity to the obedience of Christ,*
> [6] *and being ready to punish all disobedience when your obedience is fulfilled.*
> [7] *Do you look at things according to the outward appearance? If anyone is convinced in himself that he is Christ's, let him again consider this in himself, that just as he is Christ's, even so we are Christ's.* (2 Corinthians 10:4–7)

The man who thus objectifies women unquestionably has a womanizing attitude. Often, he is not above mentally or physically abusing the females he becomes involved with, since his motives for securing them in relationships are selfish and shallow and he himself is insecure. Moreover, if he is not a user and abuser of women, the man who takes his fantasies for reality is usually a romantic failure of some sort, whose self-perception is boosted only when a beautiful woman is on his arm.

IMPOSSIBLE STANDARDS

No one is good enough for these men of unrealistic and unnatural standards. Requiring that a woman be of a certain complexion, weight, height, hair style, and eye color, or that she succumb to other idiosyncrasies and personal fetishes, men in the world and in the church are rating women on biased scales of one to ten. They are seeking their mates, not for how virtuous, God-fearing, and sound of character they are, but for how these women can complement them immediately and satisfy them sexually.

The sad irony, however, is that such men are rarely the physical counterparts of the female types they idolize and set as ideals! Wanting her to be beautiful, he is often none too handsome. She must be fit and trim, but he can have an overinflated "spare tire" hanging over his belt. While she must be dressed to reveal her best features and have her makeup and hair done to perfection, he is often anything but the epitome of good grooming.

Overall, these men ask and desire of women what they themselves cannot offer. If their excessive demands are not met, they become content with the distorted fantasy images in their minds, resigning themselves to permanent, though unfulfilling, relationships with figments of their imaginations. Feeling that they cannot find an available woman who would meet their qualifications or that no suitable woman exists who fits their ideal image, they settle for being in love with themselves—sometimes in more than one unhealthy, unnatural respect.

> [27] *Likewise also the men, leaving the natural use of the woman, burned in their lust for one another, men with men committing what is shameful, and receiving in themselves the penalty of their error which was due.*
> [28] *And even as they did not like to retain God in their knowledge, God gave them over to a debased ["reprobate" KJV] mind, to do those things which are not fitting.* (Romans 1:27–28)

ONE MAN'S FANTASY: GOD'S GIFT TO WOMEN

It is with a bit of reluctance that I tell the following story. I was indirectly involved in this scenario, but it has as its central character a fellow whom I will call Dick and who happens to be a close friend of mine. This incident had its run in the church where I serve as pastor, and I only share it now because of its timely illustration of how the fantasy phenomenon plays out with men, and particularly with those men in the church. Be mindful, however, that the way in which the story's main character displayed his susceptibility to vain imaginations may not be commonly considered a situation where fantasy is an identifiable factor or cause. Nevertheless, an unexpected turn of events brought to light this individual's distorted mind-set and womanizing tendencies. Upon closer examination, his distorted, unrealistic, quixotic attitude about women became apparent, but not until he was caught.

> [23] *Be sure your sin will find you out.*
> (Numbers 32:23)

> [22] *For there is nothing hidden which will not be revealed, nor has anything been kept secret but that it should come to light.* (Mark 4:22)

Dick, the "young" man in question, was about forty-three years old when his immaturity was inadvertently displayed through his adolescent dealings with females in our church. A divorced father of four, Dick is a person I have known well for many years. In the opinions of many people, he is a hard-working, all-around good person.

Nevertheless, what was not so good about my friend and parishioner began to dawn on me during a Thanksgiving dinner event sponsored by our church last year. This was an occasion where families in and outside of the church were to be blessed with the holiday's abundance of natural harvest, an event that most attendees clearly understood to be a "dress-up" affair. Much to my embarrassment, however, Dick somehow decided that his attire would be casual. He came to the dinner dressed in jeans, sneakers, an open shirt, and a flashy gold necklace.

Needless to say, Dick's behavior angered me considerably. Not only had he openly ignored and disregarded the established dress code, but since he was a rather visible figure in the church, his status was that of a role model. In addition, he was a prominent participant in the festivities taking place that very evening!

Without biting my tongue, I confronted Dick and expressed to him my serious displeasure and disappointment in his casual attire and attitude. I relayed to him what was the general consensus of all who saw him there that night: that he looked like a young, careless teenager. "Grow up!" I angrily admonished him, before walking away. Little did I realize, however, that this brother's inappropriate dress was an external indication of a deeper, more serious, internal problem, involving a lack of accountability and responsibility on his part. And I certainly had no clue that this small incident with him was just a preview of an even greater discrepancy that would surface and erupt later on.

A few months later, however, that bigger situation reared its ugly head. To my great disappointment, several young women in the church made a general complaint to me that Dick was in the habit of making romantic overtures to each of them. According to these young ladies, who were all either in their late teens or early twenties, if Dick was not complimenting them excessively on their appearance, he was asking them overly intimate questions, extending personal invitations to private dinners, or trying to arrange meetings in other remote settings. Many times, his conversations with these young women contained inappropriate, suggestive overtones. He had even offered his personal telephone numbers to more than one girl and had paid visits to at least two of them at their workplaces.

The overall problem that these women had with Dick was twofold. First of all, while he was old enough to be their father, or at least a protective authority figure in their lives, he was choosing to flirt with them. Secondly, if he were indeed the type of man who preferred a younger woman, this might have been acceptable except for the fact that he obviously preferred younger women, plural. He refused to single out and to pursue an interest in just one of them. Instead, he was attempting to seduce all of them at the same time!

PASTORAL OVERSIGHT

Since I am the pastor of a growing and varied congregation, I try to be sensitive to and understanding of the needs of all of my parishioners, married and single. While I do emphasize to my congregation that the church is not a social club or a singles bar, it is my sincere desire to see all of my members happy, healthy, and honorably situated in the area of romance. It has never been my habit to dictate to individuals whom they could or could not entertain, date, and court as potential partners. Simply put, such is not my place or jurisdiction.

At the same time, however, God has given me the responsibility of providing a spiritual covering for the entire congregation. This often involves protecting those who do not have a covering in the natural, as with these young ladies. Thus, I occasionally have to challenge men who try to infiltrate and contaminate the church with the womanizing tactics and tendencies they employ out in the world to seduce unwitting, unfortunate females. I make no apologies for adamantly refusing to allow such behavior and practices to have free course and reign in the house of the Lord! In this case, I was absolutely compelled to confront Dick with the allegations of these young women, all of whom, again, were between the very tender ages of seventeen and twenty-four!

Prior to this incident, I had been alerted to his less-than-honorable feelings toward women, and specifically about those single women in our church. On occasion, we had openly and honestly talked about his own single status and his desire for a permanent companion. It was an issue of serious concern for my friend and brother in the Lord. He wanted and needed a wife. I had given him certain prophetic assurances that the woman God had secured for him would eventually make her appearance, and that when she did, this brother would know her immediately by the intense feelings of protectiveness he would have towards her. Desiring to make his own permanent mark in the life of this particular woman, he would not want any other men talking to her!

This utterance on my part was not made with the intent of encouraging Dick to be possessive or jealous concerning the future woman. Rather, it was given to help him to know that once she had entered his life, this woman was God's choice for him; to enable him to identify that she was indeed the one by the magnitude of his feelings; and to offer him comfort in the knowledge that waiting on the Lord would truly pay off in due time.

THE REVEALING TRUTH

Waiting, of course, was the operative word here. It was not very long before this brother gave in to impatience, doubt, and arrogance concerning single women in our church and his future possibilities with any of them. After one particularly stirring Sunday service, Dick informed me that he would never find a good woman among those in our membership, because all of the ladies there were, in his opinion, "too bossy, too independent, too demanding, or too stuck on themselves."

Again angered by his ungracious, disrespectful attitude, I asked him, in all seriousness, "Do you think that you are God's gift to women? Do you really believe you have so much to offer a female in terms of stability, good looks, and romance that none of the single women in the church is deserving, worthy, or good enough for you?" I demanded a truthful answer from him!

Immediately detecting the sarcasm in my dogmatic questioning, Dick backed down from his haughty outlook and made a desperate attempt to retrieve his negative statement through an apology. At his admission of his own imperfection, I let him alone, but from then on, I was fully alerted to and ever mindful of his unacceptable views about the opposite sex.

AN AGE-OLD QUESTION

My second cause for concern was, quite honestly, that Dick was too mature in years to have exclusive interest in girls in this youthful an age bracket. The fact of the matter was that he had been a grown man before the oldest of these young ladies was even born!

While it is true that age is only a number between many couples, it is a rare man who can properly see to the needs of a female twenty years—or more—his junior! Truthfully, I have found that in many instances where an age gap this vast (twenty years or more) exists between a man and his younger bride, the woman is robbed of much of her youth and vitality. While such thievery may not ever be intentional on the part of the husband, the loss of vibrancy and zestfulness is often a considerable one for the much younger wife, all the same.

DON JUAN IN THE CHURCH

However, my most serious concern was that Dick had been making efforts to casually court several of these women at the same time. Apparently, he was not serious about a single one of them. Such two-timing (and three-, four-, and five-timing) behavior is a definite error for any gentleman of decency and integrity, not to mention a God-fearing man! Again, the womanizer's tricks would not be tolerated in the church I had been appointed by Almighty God to spearhead! Since this type of behavior went totally against the morals of godly character, anyway, it was my obligation as this brother's friend and pastor to call him to account for his inappropriate actions. And confront him, I did.

To accomplish this task, I gathered all of the people involved together in a private, confrontational meeting, of which I was the mediator and judge. Adamant about his innocence, Dick initially denied the allegations of the young women, who accused him of certain harassment and inappropriate behavior. Actually, he did not blatantly contest the charges that he had invited them to dinner, engaged them in intimate conversation, visited their job sites, and unduly complimented them, all leveled by the several young women who sat before him.

Instead, though Dick readily admitted to having a well-known flirtatious personality, this brother argued that in trying to involve himself with all of these young women as he had, his intentions had not been romantic ones! According to him, he had no personal interest in any of the young ladies he had made overtures to. Supposedly, his multiple exchanges with them had only been friendly gestures. He held that his suggestions of private get-togethers with each of these women was in no way indicative of any romantic interest or attraction on his part. To him, it was all casual interest and a general attempt to get to know these young women better. He even went so far as to actually question their thinking in determining that he was trying to date any or all of them!

At this point in the process, I realized that Dick was not viewing the relationship dynamics between males and females realistically. I knew then he was not existing on a level of romantic maturity, but was living in a realm of sheer fantasy!

Perhaps it is really true, after all, that age is nothing but a number. One would assume that, given his forty-three years, Dick would have had enough experience to know the realities and signals of courtship. Any time a man invites a woman whom he does not already know as a friend out to dinner for just the two of them, and any time a man hands a woman his telephone number that is not on a business card or for the purpose of them discussing some professional matter together, and any time a man tells a woman that he finds her attractive and asks her personal questions about herself, such initiatives will automatically—maybe even universally—be taken as romantic gestures! Even teenagers, maturing children who are just beginning to understand and participate in the workings of love and romance, generally know this much!

Incredulously, I looked at Dick when he insisted that, all along, he had only been trying to be friendly and had not meant anything at all by his obvious flirting. I was forced to ask myself, "Is he lying, denying, or really just trying to be casual friends with all of these women? And how could he behave like this when everyone knows he is single and looking for a girlfriend or a wife, and everyone knows he is a consummate flirt, and everyone apparently knows that this type of behavior is not new to him, but is actually a part of his reputation and recent past?" I had no answers, only suspicions.

Not wanting to be overly derogatory about my friend, brother, and parishioner, I have now accepted the fact that Dick was not living in reality where it concerned his relations with and actions toward the opposite sex. I reiterate that his mind-set about male/female interactions was one etched in fantasy, where single men are free to be openly suggestive to and flirtatious with single women, and no romantic notions are to be assumed or taken by the female receiving the advances and attention. Not only did he accept that distorted notion as fact, but in the warped recesses of this brother's mind, he also believed a single man could behave in a manner that clearly expressed his personal interest toward several females simultaneously!

In handling the situation, I rebuked Dick strongly for being out of order with his inappropriate behavior toward the women in the church. I even addressed this serious issue (without mentioning names, of course) publicly to the entire congregation, so that it might serve as a lesson to all. From this experience I have learned several lessons: age does not guarantee wisdom or discretion; ignorance, whether feigned or real, causes individuals to act rather unwisely; and fantasy, when it becomes a stronghold, not only harms the individual, but also hurts everyone with whom the person comes in contact.

Brother Dick has now made the wise choice to mend his ways. At least, this is how things appear to be. Having made the proper apologies, he is now allowing himself to be steered by me, in the role of his concerned pastor and counselor, into a more respectful, gentlemanly view of females. He is learning that women are not poster girls to be looked upon for their physical attributes only, or creatures intended for the sole purpose of fulfilling men's needs and desires, or a predictable gender to be taken for granted and commonly lumped together in negative stereotypes. Neither are they an inferior half of mankind to be subdued and collected by superior-minded males!

Rather, Dick is learning what I myself have had to learn, sometimes the hard way: that every woman is a worthy being, specially crafted and designed by the Creator to birth and nurture humanity, to love and comfort one natural man, and to answer the divine call God has placed on her life. Moreover, since each woman is an individual, she is to be courted and romantically loved on an exclusive basis by one single man in her life, who is not to pursue others of her gender at the same time.

With man, it seems, the very idea of his being able to handle two (or more) women at one time is his biggest fantasy. But the notion that such is acceptable in the eyes of God, or even with society, is actually an intolerable and inexcusable fallacy.

Part 3

Fruitless Relationships:

When Loving You Is Wrong, but I'm Convinced That It's Right

Fruitless Relationships:

When Loving You Is Wrong, but I'm Convinced That It's Right

*T*he broad pattern for our lives, as planned and expressed by God from the very beginning of creation, is that we *"be fruitful and multiply"* (Genesis 1:28) in the context of sanctioned relationships. Ever since then, relationships, just like individuals, have produced fruit. Whether the resulting produce is good and nutritious or rotten and tainted is determined by the integrity of the relationship and of the people involved.

> [43] *A good tree does not bear bad fruit, nor does a bad tree bear good fruit.*
> [44] *For every tree is known by its own fruit. For men do not gather figs from thorns, nor do they gather grapes from a bramble bush.*

> [45] *A good man out of the good treasure of his heart brings forth good; and an evil man out of the evil treasure of his heart brings forth evil. For out of the abundance of the heart his mouth speaks.*
>
> (Luke 6:43–45)

Fruitless relationships are barren in the sense that they fail to produce good fruit, even when the affected parties expend long and arduous efforts to generate the desired results of fulfillment and happiness. Because these relationships are outlawed by God, when they are illicitly engaged in, they are rooted in evil and can do nothing but bear bad fruit. Inevitably, dire consequences do arise, causing considerable pain and heartache for everyone concerned.

Severely disappointing, these futile alliances are doomed to complete destruction because of the lack of wisdom in undertaking them and the evil results of engaging in them. Our Lord will not long tolerate barren relationships or the production of bad fruit in the lives of His own children. He Himself will deal with them by taking a sharp knife and cutting them out, if He must.

> [10] *And even now the ax is laid to the root of the trees. Therefore every tree which does not bear good fruit is cut down and thrown into the fire.*
>
> (Matthew 3:10)

> [2] *Every branch in Me that does not bear fruit He takes away; and every branch that bears fruit He prunes, that it may bear more fruit.* (John 15:2)

One of the clearest evidences of an entrenched relational stronghold is when a person insists that a relationship is right and blessed by God, no matter what the Bible or anyone else may say to the contrary. The defiant attitude that says, "You can tell me all you want that my relationship is wrong, but you'll never convince me because I know it's right," gives immediate indication of a deceitful stronghold having been established. It is plainly a relationship in which the individual speaking the sentiment is somehow bound to another with unwholesome ties, at best, or by total depravity, at worst.

Somehow the person has convinced himself that what is wrong is right, accepting the distorted lie of the Enemy rather than the truth of God's Word. Ordinarily, we open ourselves up to this kind of self-deception when we do not expose ourselves to the light of the Son and fail to spend enough quality time in intimate relationship with Him and His truth.

> [6] *If we say that we have fellowship with Him, and walk in darkness, we lie and do not practice the truth.*
> [7] *But if we walk in the light as He is in the light, we have fellowship with one another, and the blood of Jesus Christ His Son cleanses us from all sin.*
> [8] *If we say that we have no sin, we deceive ourselves, and the truth is not in us.* (1 John 1:6–8)

To disentangle oneself from the bondage of self-deceit and the snare of fruitless relationships, an individual must admit the truth to himself and to God that his personal connections with these deceptive strongholds and ties to the forbidden are indeed sinful, repent of the sin, and receive God's forgiveness and cleansing. Only by clearing out the debris of corrupt living can room be made for fruitful, fulfilling relationships.

6

Cursed Be the Ties That Bind

M r. Goodbar is representative of whatever an individual considers to be an ideal relationship partner. Quite often, however, after a person has searched for and established a Mr. Goodbar-type relationship, he or she has difficulty in officially ending that alliance once it has gone sour. This internal and external resistance is due to the still-intact soul tie.

Simply speaking, a soul tie is a bond that is formed between two individuals' souls and that knits them together mentally, emotionally, and psychologically. These bonds develop in the realm of the soul, the Greek word for which is *psuche* or *psyche,* from which we derive our word *psychology* (the study of the human soul or mind).

Depending on the underlying nature of the bonds that form it, a soul tie can be either a blessing or a disaster. The Bible gives us as examples the following situations of a close friendship, fellow army comrades, and the members of the body of Christ in which soul-tie bonds have had and can have beneficial effects for the parties involved:

> [1] *Now when he had finished speaking to Saul, the soul of Jonathan was knit to the soul of David, and Jonathan loved him as his own soul.*
> [2] *Saul took him that day, and would not let him go home to his father's house anymore.*
> [3] *Then Jonathan and David made a covenant, because he loved him as his own soul.*
> [4] *And Jonathan took off the robe that was on him and gave it to David, with his armor, even to his sword and his bow and his belt.* (1 Samuel 18:1–4)

> [11] *So all the men of Israel were gathered against the city, knit together as one man.*
> (Judges 20:11 KJV)

> [2] *Their hearts may be encouraged, being knit together in love, and attaining to all riches of the full assurance of understanding, to the knowledge of the mystery of God, both of the Father and of Christ.*
> [18] *Let no one cheat you of your reward, taking delight in false humility and worship of angels, intruding into those things which he has not seen, vainly puffed up by his fleshly mind,*
> [19] *and not holding fast to the Head, from whom all the body, nourished and knit together by joints and ligaments, grows with the increase that is from God.* (Colossians 2:2, 18–19)

> [15] *Speaking the truth in love, [we] may grow up in all things into Him who is the head; Christ;*
> [16] *from whom the whole body, joined and knit together by what every joint supplies, according to the effective working by which every part does its share, causes growth of the body for the edifying of itself in love.* (Ephesians 4:15–16)

The unity of purpose created by positive soul ties can bring about victory over a common enemy, individual and relational growth, and an increase of love, protection, edification, and encouragement for one another.

THE BOND OF SEXUAL INTIMACY

God desires that the strongest and most intimate relationship any of His children have with another human being be the marriage union. Because He designed marriage as the foundation for all the rest of societal structures, the marital unit, of necessity, needs to have the most integral strength so that it can stand up under the negative pressures and forces of this world.

To help form and fortify the bond between a husband and a wife, and thus strengthen their marriage, God created the most effective glue known—sexual intimacy. Sex was designed by God not just as the means of producing offspring, but more basically as the bonding agent to unite two individuals together on all levels, body-to-body, soul-to-soul, and spirit-to-spirit.

> [24] *Therefore a man shall leave his father and mother and be joined to his wife, and they shall become one flesh.* (Genesis 2:24)

God designed sex to be very pleasurable physically and emotionally so that it would have an addictive quality to it. The better a behavior makes us feel, the more we repeat it; so the more a couple engages in the delights and pleasures of sexual intimacy, the more the soul tie between them is intensified and the stronger the marriage bond becomes. Because sexual intimacy exponentially reinforces the soul-tie bonds between the partners, sexual relations are to be kept strictly within the confines of the marriage union.

> [4] *Marriage is honorable among all, and the bed undefiled; but fornicators and adulterers God will judge.* (Hebrews 13:4)

God isn't the cruel Judge that some think He is. After all, He is the Designer of our sexuality in the first place. He just designates the boundaries, for our good.

THE BONDAGE OF NEGATIVE SOUL TIES

Just as soul ties can produce powerful positive effects, they can also lead to disaster if they are formed outside of God's will and intentions. An incident in the Old Testament sheds light on the strength of unity that can arise from the formation of soul ties.

> [1] *Now the whole earth had one language and one speech.*
> [4] *And they said, "Come, let us build ourselves a city, and a tower whose top is in the heavens; let us make a name for ourselves, lest we be scattered abroad over the face of the whole earth."*
> [5] *But the LORD came down to see the city and the tower which the sons of men had built.*
> [6] *And the LORD said, "Indeed the people are one and they all have one language, and this is what they begin to do; now nothing that they propose to do will be withheld from them.*
> [7] *"Come, let Us go down and there confuse their language, that they may not understand one another's speech."*
> [8] *So the LORD scattered them abroad from there over the face of all the earth, and they ceased building the city.*   (Genesis 11:1, 4–8)

As the people at Babel joined together with one purpose in mind—to thwart the will of God that they be spread out over the face of the earth—they were in such accord that the Lord declared they could have anything they went after, even if it was contrary to His will. Such is the united power inherent in the bond of soul ties, whether it is used for good or for ill.

The circumstances of April, the woman who was featured in a previous chapter on fantasy relationships, readily illustrate what a negative soul tie is. She was in bondage to the mostly imagined romantic relationship she envisioned with her boss. Even though she had not physically joined herself to her boss, she had formed a definite mental and emotional bond to him in the arena of her soul. This bond produced evil fruit in her life.

Any bond that arises from forbidden relationships or causes harmful effects becomes bondage to the persons who are involved. A mind-set that says, "Loving you is wrong, but I'm convinced that it's right," signals that a negative soul tie has been established. Clearly, the individual who expresses such a fallacy is somehow bound in a detrimental relationship or to someone who is off-limits. The knowledge of the illegality of this relationship is also apparent in the confession, "Loving you is wrong." Although not always the case, the forbidden act that usually ties the knot between two souls is sexual intimacy.

As commanded by the Bible, sex outside of marriage is illegal, and breaking this law can have phenomenal repercussions. Sexual involvement can form such an entangling web of soul ties that certain relationships became nearly impossible to break away from and discontinue. Like powerful, mature tree roots, the tentacles from multiple soul ties can often reach deep into an individual's personality and spirit and become a part of his or her very being.

THE EFFECTS OF PROMISCUITY

Furthermore, when promiscuous sex is engaged in, the soul of the practicing individual becomes divided and subsequently gets scattered among the multiple partners who have existed. This may appear to be especially true where women are concerned, because soul ties are so emotionally binding and women are particularly susceptible in the area of emotions. Thus, women have trouble severing the emotional cords to their sexual partners and will often attempt to reestablish the emotional bonds, no matter how detrimental they may be. However, the Bible declares that men are just as bound to their previous sex partners, even though it might not be as readily apparent because men tend not to exhibit the emotionalism women do about the breakup of an affair.

> [16] *Do you not know that he who is joined to a harlot is one body with her? For "the two," He says, "shall become one flesh."* (1 Corinthians 6:16)

Men are often so strongly tied to their prior liaisons in their visual and physical memories that they will habitually try to reconsummate the sexual encounters.

Frequently, the souls of persons who have been promiscuous in sex are drawn to those of all their previous partners, even long after the relationships have ended. This can happen to such an extent that when these persons marry, they often develop sexual and communication problems with their mates.

HOW PERVERSE SPIRITS OPERATE

Concerning forbidden relationships marked by strongholds and soul ties, homosexual relationships are very likely characterized by the most perverse, most deeply entrenched bondage of any prohibited alliance. How this sexual deviation and the resulting abominable lifestyle develop merits our investigation. You see, many of these ungodly relationships are the direct result of a past homosexual molestation. This involves the transfer of the homosexual spirit through a soul tie. The spirit of homosexuality and the ties that bind it to an individual are so strong that few are able to completely break free from this enslavement without deliverance in the spiritual and emotional realms and ongoing counseling to reinforce new habits and behaviors.

Homosexuality is not the only spirit that can be transferred through the soul tie after sexual intimacy. Greed, unfaithfulness, lust for power and wealth, and many other ungodly spirits can also be transmitted through physical intimacy.

SEDUCING SPIRITS

Within the realm of the church, great men of God can attest to the attack of seducing spirits. In particular, pastors can easily relay horror stories about women in their congregations who have practically thrown themselves sexually at their spiritual leaders. These leaders do not need to be physically attractive, wealthy, or even charming. The women are simply being used by seducing spirits, who have received their assignments from Satan, to secure the downfalls of targeted church leaders.

Because Satan himself cannot openly or directly attack God's people, he commissions these women, who have been previously defiled in their spirits by the Enemy, to lure the elders, pastors, and ministers into compromising positions. If a man of God falls prey to the seduction, a soul tie will have been established. Satan is then able to freely transfer all manner of defilement to the spiritual leader through the bonds formed with the seductress. Ultimately, these attacks undermine and destroy the work of God, the reputations and ministries of these Christian leaders, and the faith of many believers.

UNDOING THE KNOT

After the knitting together of souls in an illegal rendezvous has taken place, a spiritual untying is required for deliverance. The Word of God tells us that we have the power both to bind and to loose.

> [19] *And I will give you the keys of the kingdom of heaven, and whatever you bind on earth will be bound in heaven, and whatever you loose on earth will be loosed in heaven.* (Matthew 16:19)

It is of great necessity that we loose every knot that has been illegally tied in our lives. The knitting together of two souls done within a marriage can bring forth good fruit. However, any illicit ties or knots made with Mr.

Goodbar need to be broken. Pray the following prayer and believe in your heart that it will result in your being loosed from the snare of the soul tie.

> Heavenly Father,
>
> In the name of Jesus, I submit all of my soul, my body, my desires, and my emotions to You and Your Spirit. I denounce any conscious or subconscious attachments formed in my past: past involvements, past emotional attachments, and past premarital sexual relationships. I denounce the emotional, physical, and spiritual ties formed by my involvement in any forbidden sexual, mental, or emotional intimacy outside of my marriage. I confess all of my ungodly spirit, soul, and body ties as sin. I thank You for forgiving me and cleansing me of all unrighteousness, right now!
>
> I loose myself from all soulish ties to past sexual partners and ungodly relationships. Please uproot all connections through sexual bondage, sexual deviations, emotional longings, dependencies, perversions, and enslaving thoughts and fantasies. I bind every evil spirit that reinforced the soul tie and any evil transference into my life through ungodly associations.
>
> Lord, I ask You to cleanse my soul and to erase totally from my memory bank all illicit unions that I participated in. Set me free so that I may serve only the purposes of God and my mate.
>
> Father, now that I have asked You this and know it is in accordance with Your will for my life, I believe I am totally forgiven and set free. I recommit myself to You and my mate, in Jesus' name.   Amen

If you prayed this prayer with genuineness and sincerity, you are now starting a clean slate with God and your spouse. If you are not yet married, get ready for an explosively wonderful relationship. Further, as much as you are able, proceed to kick the Devil out of Mr. Goodbar and live the God-kind of life for which you were chosen from now on!

7

But the Water Is Bad

*H*omosexuality and perversion, which we are now going to examine, are touchy and controversial topics in the sensitive, increasingly liberal spheres of society. However, they are even more taboo within the righteous realms of the church. Unrealistically, we have embraced the illusion that the church is perfect. We expect it to be free of the ills of the world, when, in fact, it is only made up of imperfect people from society who tend to bring their social and personal problems with them into the pews. In my opinion, the issues of homosexuality and sexual perversion, particularly as they relate to Christendom, are ones that need to be addressed and handled with more directness than discretion, with more power than political correctness, with more antipathy than acceptance, and with more Word than words.

The Scriptures state very clearly what homosexuality and other perversions are, how God views them, and why these sinful practices are manifested in the world:

[18] *For the wrath of God is revealed from heaven against all ungodliness and unrighteousness of men, who suppress the truth in unrighteousness,*
[19] *because what may be known of God is manifest in them, for God has shown it to them.*
[20] *For since the creation of the world His invisible attributes are clearly seen, being understood by the things that are made, even His eternal power and Godhead, so that they are without excuse,*
[21] *because, although they knew God, they did not glorify Him as God, nor were thankful, but became futile in their thoughts, and their foolish hearts were darkened.*
[22] *Professing to be wise, they became fools,*
[23] *and changed the glory of the incorruptible God into an image made like corruptible man; and birds and four-footed animals and creeping things.*
[24] *Therefore God also gave them up to uncleanness, in the lusts of their hearts, to dishonor their bodies among themselves,*
[25] *who exchanged the truth of God for the lie, and worshiped and served the creature rather than the Creator, who is blessed forever. Amen.*
[26] *For this reason God gave them up to vile passions. For even their women exchanged the natural use for what is against nature.*
[27] *Likewise also the men, leaving the natural use of the woman, burned in their lust for one another, men with men committing what is shameful, and receiving in themselves the penalty of their error which was due.*
[28] *And even as they did not like to retain God in their knowledge, God gave them over to a debased mind, to do those things which are not fitting;*
[29] *being filled with all unrighteousness, sexual immorality, wickedness, covetousness, maliciousness; full of envy, murder, strife, deceit, evil-mindedness; they are whisperers,*
[32] *who, knowing the righteous judgment of God, that those who practice such things are deserving of death, not only do the same but also approve of those who practice them.*   (Romans 1:18–29, 32)

THE REPROACH OF HOMOSEXUALITY

In the book of Genesis, we find the Bible's first recorded incident of homosexual activity, as practiced by the wicked men of Sodom and Gomorrah:

> [1] *Now the two angels came to Sodom in the evening, and Lot was sitting in the gate of Sodom. When Lot saw them, he rose to meet them, and he bowed himself with his face toward the ground.*
> [2] *And he said, "Here now, my lords, please turn in to your servant's house and spend the night, and wash your feet; then you may rise early and go on your way." And they said, "No, but we will spend the night in the open square."*
> [3] *But he insisted strongly; so they turned in to him and entered his house. Then he made them a feast, and baked unleavened bread, and they ate.*
> [4] *Now before they lay down, the men of the city, the men of Sodom, both old and young, all the people from every quarter, surrounded the house.*
> [5] *And they called to Lot and said to him, "Where are the men who came to you tonight? Bring them out to us that we may know them carnally."*
> [6] *So Lot went out to them through the doorway, shut the door behind him,*
> [7] *and said, "Please, my brethren, do not do so wickedly!*
> [8] *"See now, I have two daughters who have not known a man; please, let me bring them out to you, and you may do to them as you wish; only do nothing to these men, since this is the reason they have come under the shadow of my roof."*
> [9] *And they said, "Stand back!" Then they said, "This one came in to stay here, and he keeps acting as a judge; now we will deal worse with you than with them." So they pressed hard against the man Lot, and came near to break down the door.*
> [10] *But the men reached out their hands and pulled Lot into the house with them, and shut the door.*
> [11] *And they struck the men who were at the doorway*

of the house with blindness, both small and great,
so that they became weary trying to find the door.
(Genesis 19:1–11)

Our words *sodomy* and *sodomite* were obviously derived from Sodom, the name of the city where these detestable activities regularly took place. Sodomy is defined as "sexual intercourse with a member of the same sex or with an animal, especially anal copulation; an unnatural sexual relationship." Put plainly and simply, it is the primary and most noted sexual practice of males under the abominable curse of homosexuality, a sinful reproach that includes the practice of lesbianism, as well.

Since the mid-eighties, societal acceptance of homosexuality has steadily grown, especially in the United States. We read about and see its bold, blatant practitioners in all facets of the media, including popular print, respected radio formats, successful sitcoms, and especially on trash talk shows. If it is not men with men or women with women being celebrated and paraded before us, then it is the exhibitions and explanations of vile variations and damnable deviations of the homosexual spirit, such as drag queens, cross-dressers, transvestites, transsexuals, and bisexuals. Some of these female men and male women have even become lauded pop icons, possessing large, faithful followings.

Even the United States government is joining in the free-for-all festivities. Slowly but surely, our country is weakening her written-law strongholds against sexual sins, simultaneously reinterpreting and re-laying the foundation of "In God we trust." We can see her arms of acceptance widening in our military ranks, as well, where undisclosed homosexuals have always quietly fought the physical war, but are now vocally fighting for civil rights. "Don't ask, don't tell" has become the current command. Likewise, the libraries and classrooms of our public school systems have been infiltrated with the lessons of pro-gay literature; bearing titles such as *My*

Other Mommy and *Jack Has Two Fathers,* such material is not uncommon in the primary grades.

INVADING THE CHURCH

Sadly, the clergy has also abandoned the steadfast biblical stance against sin in whatever form and has instead embraced the ideology that says, "God made us as we are, so we are all right as we are." Not only are gay men and women being allowed the rights and privileges of active church membership, they are also securing church offices and holding leadership positions, including pastorates. Same-sex marriage ceremonies are being performed regularly within the sacred walls of worship.

Even harder to ignore is the shameful sexual stigma of the church itself, some denominations of which have been particularly noted for rampant sexual sin and impropriety for generations. We have all read headlines featuring the sad stories of church members' accusations of rape and molestation against their Sunday school teachers, pastors, and other church leaders. In these cases, homosexuality may not have always been the particular offense. However, the spirit of perversion is the common father of all sexual sin, and these are all of the same unclean spirit.

Also ever-surfacing are the twisted tales of Catholic priests' illicit, perverse affairs with young boys and the emotional ramifications these innocent children suffer. The Protestant church is not exempt either, as it is currently being bombarded with lawsuits citing sexual misconduct in which sodomitic activity is a noted offense.

Of no less concern are the issues of those professed Christians who have failed to confess to God the sexual sins, misconduct, and violations of their pasts, as victims and/or perpetrators. If these people do not fully submit their former lusts and activities to Jesus, and if their sins remain covered with something other than the blood of

Christ, these problem areas are certain to resurface and wreak havoc in their lives.

Tragically, for each of the many so-called Christians who are practicing the sin of homosexuality, a multiplied number of believers exist who refuse to confront this issue forcefully or even believe it is one that affects Christ's church. I am shocked that you are shocked when I declare that this sin and other perversions are indeed occurring within the confines of the church, and that they are absolutely wrong to be going on in the first place. I am shocked by those of you who refuse to acknowledge the stench of this "bad water" flowing freely, poisoning, polluting, and perverting the vessels of Christians everywhere.

> [19] *If you have not gone astray to uncleanness...be free from this bitter water that brings a curse.*
> (Numbers 5:19)

I am also appalled at those convicted church leaders who are aware of what is happening but who are not actively striving to rid their church members of this deadly, infectious disease. They may be passive in dealing with this situation either because of outright denial of the vaccination—God's Word—or due to a lack of knowledge. To those who are uninformed about the biblical mandates against homosexuality, I offer the following:

> [13] *If a man lies with a male as he lies with a woman, both of them have committed an abomination. They shall surely be put to death. Their blood shall be upon them.* (Leviticus 20:13)

> [22] *You shall not lie with a male as with a woman. It is an abomination.* (Leviticus 18:22)

> [9] *Do you not know that the unrighteous will not inherit the kingdom of God? Do not be deceived. Neither fornicators, nor idolaters, nor adulterers, nor homosexuals, nor sodomites,*

[10] *nor thieves, nor covetous, nor drunkards, nor re-*
vilers, nor extortioners will inherit the kingdom of
God.   (1 Corinthians 6:9–10)

If we agree that the Word of God is to be our life-long how-to manual for daily Christian living, how can we not regard its most plainspoken instructions? Why do we dare attempt to twist, reinterpret, misinterpret, or totally ignore its holy commandments for our lives? How is it that we can claim to know the meaning and purpose of Christ's salvation, yet disagree with the Author's definition of it, or disobey the Owner's orders regarding the keeping of it? And what are the explanations for this sudden, focused attention regarding homosexuality that we are witnessing both in society and in the sanctuary?

I am convinced that purposeful, deliberate, satanic forces are the evil culprits behind this recent forefront exposure of homosexuality and other sexual sins. These demonic principalities are taking crucial action to place sexual perversion in the public spotlight, not with the intent that such acts be condemned and criticized, but to ensure that they are practiced, paraded, promoted, popularized, and protected by an ever-growing discipleship. More and more notable, respected people, famous and ordinary people, "Christian" people—doctors, lawyers, teachers, preachers, husbands, wives, and teenagers—are "coming out" of their closets of shame, bringing their dirty laundry with them and airing it with public pride. Unfortunately, the Congress of the United States, under the legal guise of having to protect the civil rights of others, is making it increasingly difficult for us to exercise our right to cry aloud against this sin, as we see it.

But take a stand we must. Just as the Prince of Darkness is desperate and determined to expand his hellish domain with the lost souls of the sexually perverted, so must we take on the strength of our salvation and uplift our heavenly Father's kingdom through the powerful preaching of deliverance.

FREEDOM FROM BONDAGE

I believe that deliverance is available for those under the curse and stronghold of homosexuality.

> [11] *And such* [including homosexuals, sodomites, and fornicators] *were some of you. But you were washed, but you were sanctified, but you were justified in the name of the Lord Jesus and by the Spirit of our God.* (1 Corinthians 6:11)

If the Corinthian believers were no longer under the satanic bondages they had been subject to, then true liberty and deliverance are available to today's Christians also. The Scriptures reassure us that *"if we confess our sins, He is faithful and just to forgive us our sins and to cleanse us from all unrighteousness"* (1 John 1:9). After confession, forgiveness, conversion, and the mind-healing power of God have been instituted, the previously afflicted individual must make a complete change of lifestyle, coupled with regular counseling, in order to prevent the return of the former filthy spirits.

While some studies have attempted to show that individuals are born with homosexual tendencies, others argue that conditioning and environment determine sexual orientation. I am convinced, however, that all sexual sin is fostered through the spirit of perversion, a foul demon, and that the majority of homosexual individuals have been demonically attacked in the womb or during their very early years, perhaps through the authority of a generational curse.

Nevertheless, *"in all these things we are more than conquerors through Him who loved us"* (Romans 8:37). Through this we realize that there exists no force in hell or on earth, in the natural elements or in the spiritual realm, in the body or in the mind, that the powers of heaven cannot and will not break on our behalf or subdue for our benefit, if we love God. It is through this awesome assurance and powerful protection, then, that the former slave to sexual sin—and every single one of us, in fact, because we have all been slaves to sin of one sort or another—is set free to walk with complete confidence in the newness of life.

> ⁴ *Even so we also should walk in newness of life.*
> ¹⁷ *But God be thanked that though you were slaves of sin, yet you obeyed from the heart that form of doctrine to which you were delivered.*
> ¹⁸ *And having been set free from sin, you became slaves of righteousness.*   (Romans 6:4, 17–18)

THE DISTORTED POWER OF PERVERSION

The Greek and Hebrew words that are translated in the Bible as various forms of the English word *perversion* also mean "confusion, distortion, an unnatural mixture (incest, sodomy, and bestiality), wickedness, corruption, falseness, crookedness, being twisted." (For you KJV readers, the now archaic word *froward* was often used to translate the Hebrew word for *perverted*.) The Scriptures tell us that there is such a thing as a perverse spirit and that it creates powerful evil effects when unleashed:

> ¹⁴ *The LORD has mingled a perverse spirit* ["a spirit of distortion" NAS] *in* [Egypt's] *midst; and they have caused Egypt to err in all her work, as a drunken man staggers in his vomit.* (Isaiah 19:14)

> ⁴ *A wholesome tongue is a tree of life, but perverseness in it breaks the spirit.*   (Proverbs 15:4)

> ²⁸ *A perverse man spreads strife, and a slanderer separates intimate friends.*   (Proverbs 16:28 NAS)

People with this perverse spirit have either opened themselves up to its attack through their sinful behavior or have been cursed by someone else, perhaps generationally through inheritance from their natural bloodline. No matter how this demonic spirit gained the right to attack, eventually the person becomes so corrupted and twisted that his entire life—body, mind, and soul— becomes perverted. God finds this evil spirit detestable and abhorrent:

> [20] *Those who are of a perverse heart are an abomination to the LORD.* (Proverbs 11:20)

VICTIMIZED BY PERVERSITY

The following is a true story of an innocent child who was gripped by the clutches of the vile, foul, demonic spirit of perversion.

Mae, a friendly, twenty-nine-year-old divorcée asked a young, twelve-year-old neighbor boy to run errands for her on several occasions. The favors involved picking up groceries, helping with the laundry, and other small but tedious tasks. She asked the lad to help so frequently that an affectionate bond grew between them.

Recently divorced, Mae was still in great pain over the desertion of her husband. It took everything she had to keep the psychological demons that were plaguing her at bay, as they slowly tried to prod her over the edge of the cliff into the abyss of insanity.

Seeking a means by which to put her life in perspective, Mae turned to the sweet, understanding twelve-year-old lad. The two of them were a study in opposites: she was an adult, he was a youth; she was wise and experienced, he was vulnerable and innocent; she was a woman, he was a boy.

While the relationship between the boy and the woman had always been a friendly, affectionate one, the boy began to notice that the casual hugs and kisses they shared were slowly evolving into intimate caresses. Mae's lingering hugs were becoming increasingly more familiar, as her kisses were getting closer and closer to his lips.

What would happen to this young boy over a two-year period of time would affect him long after he had become a man. Out of her own neediness and immaturity, Mae had robbed the boy of his innocence. Unlocking his passions at too early an age, she thrust him into manhood prematurely, a manhood that happened to be only an illusion. After his manly passions had kicked in and were satisfied by his neighbor, he would immediately revert to his boyhood nature, playing with toy trucks and jingling marbles in his pockets.

Although he was a still a child and often returned to childish things, the sexuality of the lad had been awakened. He could never fully recover his former state of innocence. No longer did he prefer girls his own age. In later years, after the boy had officially reached manhood, he suffered problems that stemmed from the early exposure and sexual perversion of his past. Womanizing tendencies and a degenerate, lawless rebelliousness were just two of the tragic side effects he suffered.

THE SPIRIT BEHIND PERVERSION

As previously stated, perversion is a demonic spirit that needs to be exposed. It is a virus as common as the common cold and as deadly as the AIDS virus, through which it claims more victims than any other disease. Some of perversion's evil manifestations are the whole spectrum of sexually transmitted diseases from herpes to chlamydia to gonorrhea, all of which target the female reproductive system with particular viciousness.

Perversion is not a respecter of persons, claiming victims of both sexes, from every region, of all races, of every age, and from all backgrounds. Its lusts are expressed through the life of a sexually perverted individual and can only be satisfied through the imprisonment or total annihilation of that individual. Most significantly, however, the only way this powerful spirit can be overcome is through the saving blood of Jesus Christ as it is received into the victim's perverted heart and cleanses him from every effect of sin.

> ⁵ *To Him who loved us and washed us from our sins in His own blood.* (Revelation 1:5)

> ¹¹ *And such* [homosexuals, sodomites, and other perverse persons] *were some of you. But you were washed, but you were sanctified, but you were justified in the name of the Lord Jesus and by the Spirit of our God.* (1 Corinthians 6:11)

Dear reader, I caution you to *"keep your heart with all diligence"* (Proverbs 4:23) so that you may never become entangled in the wicked web of the spirit of perversion. However, if you have already become ensnared, I pray that you will find true deliverance through our Lord Jesus Christ. And, remember, *"If the Son makes you free, you shall be free indeed"* (John 8:36).

8

The World's Greatest Lover

*I*n concluding the topic of fruitless relationships, I want to relay to you the personal story of a believer rescued from the emotional grasp of a nonproductive relationship and restored to the perfect will of God. June's testimony is one of nearly falling into, yet narrowly escaping from, the Tempter's snare. This escape, which she found only in Christ Jesus, brought victory to her life and a sweet deliverance that has reached beyond the particular hold of her fruitless affair. Withstanding temptation, her faith gave her power to resist the lure to act selfishly in love, the enticement to commit adultery, the appeal of the forbidden, and the potential addiction to an ultimately unnecessary relationship.

Read June's story with the *"eyes of your understanding"* (Ephesians 1:18), listen with your spiritual ears, and be inspired to end your own barren, fruitless union. Then you will again be able to walk in the positive, productive will of God.

OVERCOMING THE OVERWHELMING

As a young girl, I had a very difficult home life, filled with abuse, rejection, hatred, and confusion. Thus, throughout my teenage years and young adulthood, I painfully searched for identity, peace, and love in all the wrong places. In the process, I fell prey to a host of young men who used and abused my body and broke my spirit. Tormented and insecure after years of being violated and misused, I was desperate for genuine love.

Then, one memorable, blessed day, I met the man of my dreams: His name was Jesus. He was as gentle, kind, and loving toward me as the previous men in my life had been violent, uncaring, and disrespectful. He promised me that He would never leave me and that He would always take care of me. He reminded me that even in times past, when I was a young girl in such emotional pain, I had often felt His presence in the midst of all my suffering.

Jesus and I were virtually inseparable—at least it was that way until the time when I met and married a natural man. Harry seemed to have been designed just for me. He was the companion, friend, and lover I had been praying for. I wholeheartedly thanked Jesus for blessing me with a man who would finally make me feel complete. With my new husband, I knew I would at long last be a happy woman.

I had always longed to have not only the perfect husband, but also the ideal family, a family totally different from the one in which I had grown up. Upon being married, I planned to start and establish this family of my dreams with Harry.

It was not long, however, before my marriage became less than ideal. My vision of family was not one shared by my spouse. Because of that, Harry and I grew increasingly distant. I felt betrayed, having believed marriage and children were what my husband wanted

114

also. Although I loved Harry very much, I began to feel less certain of his love for me. The difficult issue of what we each wanted and expected from marriage gave rise to a multitude of other arguments and controversies between us, including my troubled past. After years of not resolving these troubling conflicts, we became a divided household.

REMEMBERING MY FIRST LOVE

At especially difficult moments in this painful period, I would think about my first true love, Jesus, and realize how much I missed our closeness. It had been a long time since I had prayed a really sincere prayer or made any heartfelt confession to Him, but I knew He still loved me. I just was not so sure that I had been loving Him as I should, because I was well aware of my almost complete abandonment of Him since I had married Harry. After taking my marriage vows, I had let Jesus slip into the background, making Him more of a last-minute resort than my day-to-day Guide. And now that I was preoccupied with the problems in my marriage, I still was not seeking His help!

During this difficult time, it never really occurred to me that I was living beneath my Christian privilege. Instead of running to Jesus as I had a right and need to do, I was trying to ease the turmoil in my life on my own. Not only that, but I was slowly, surely allowing earthly concerns to cause me to disregard my spiritual needs.

It was at this point in my life, with my old insecurities resurfacing and my feelings of failure as a wife and dedicated Christian growing daily, that a totally unexpected event took place: I met a new man—a wonderful new man. Suddenly, incredibly, he was there. Just in my professional circle at first, without warning he became a part of my personal life. A truly genuine individual, he made me feel needed, loved, and important again, almost without effort. An affectionate, sensitive, loving man, he regularly told me that I was all of these things. In his shining presence, I felt that anything was possible for me. From the moment he came into my life, things that had previously mattered so much seemed insignificant.

More and more, our friendship grew. And, it felt so right. Before long, it was an undeniable, although highly classified, relationship: my husband, family, and colleagues never knew. For any other two people, this might have been a totally positive thing, a green light to become further or permanently involved. But for us, a couple of serious problems existed—our respective spouses. The reality that we both were married was a great concern for each of us.

BECOMING ENMESHED

Yet, in spite of all this, we continued in our forbidden flirtations and allowed the inevitable to happen: we fell in love. Despite our vows of lifelong fidelity to our mates, we allowed our mutually friendly feelings to evolve into serious affection. Love from a natural man had never been so readily available to me, not even from my husband, Harry. Likewise, when I was in his company, he exuded adoration for me, something I had never felt before or had even known was possible to experience. I lived on cloud nine when we were together and fantasized about our next meeting when we were apart.

This man assured me of all the things I had so desperately needed to hear and more desperately needed to believe about myself. Always cherishing me and treating me with utmost respect, he became the protector and emotional provider I had always longed for. Even more important to me, although he had no children, he had the definite signs of being a great family man and father. We often discussed our future life together, which he wanted to include children. And so, I was hooked.

CONVICTION AND SELF-JUSTIFICATION

Well, almost hooked. As a born-again Christian, I could not help but feel incredible conviction and sometimes outright condemnation over my behavior. As a saved man, he felt the same nagging, stabbing prick in his conscience. In an effort to suppress and deny my guilt, I sought both justification for and an understanding of my involvement with him. The intelligent part of me would not allow the rest of me to blame it all on my husband. I knew that marriage was a two-way street and that I had some scary skeletons in my emotional closet, too.

Nor could I resolve what appeared to be my out-of-character actions. What was wrong with me? I had always been a loyal person and would never do anything to deliberately hurt or harm anyone, especially not the man to whom I had committed my life. I had always despised, and sometimes openly disdained, women who even dared to hold a lengthy conversation with a married man, let alone fall in love with him! And here I was, practicing what I had once so forcefully condemned.

However, this was not really the issue. Since hindsight is perfect, I can now see that temptation had come my way and that I was speedily falling for it. A trial of my faith in God and faithfulness to my husband had come, and I was failing the test.

Satan knew that there was not only a void in my marriage relationship, but that there was an even greater hole in my personal esteem. And God had given him permission to tempt me in this, my weakest area. Up to that point, had I been more in tune with my first love, Jesus, I might not have even taken a second glance at my new Mr. Right. However, knowing what my emotional needs and desires were, Satan began to entice me with the presence of this new man and what looked like another chance—after so many previous failures—for a fantastic relationship.

117

Relationships, after all, had always been my downfall. I now see that the unfruitful one I had begun sharing with this man was part of a long-established pattern. I thought he was meeting my emotional needs, but in actuality, he was probably only encouraging my dependency and neediness. Because of his genuine love, though, he never realized this. All the same, it was up to me to figure out that there were unresolved issues in my life that only Jesus and I could work through and overcome together. Further, I had to learn patience and the art of waiting on God instead of habitually looking outside His will for answers.

THE HEAT GETS TURNED UP

Back then, however, while in the actual throes of temptation, I was seriously struggling. Our relationship had become increasingly intense. Although it was an exclusively emotional affair, the issue of my extramarital love was weighing heavily upon my spiritual conscience. Not only was the task of hiding my secret love from my husband becoming increasingly difficult as my feelings grew, but my passionate resolve to refrain from taking that ultimate step into undisputed adultery was weakening daily. With our emotional ties becoming stronger, it was harder for us to remain apart. We both knew it would be only a matter of time before something irreversible happened.

Simultaneously, I did and did not want to cross that final threshold of physical intimacy with this man. In direct opposition to what my emotions were suggesting, the Holy Spirit was constantly reminding me that my body was the temple of the Lord. While my loving another man was indeed a violation of my marriage commitment, I still desperately wanted to hold on to the last shred of marital and spiritual dignity I possessed. So, I resisted the consummation of what I knew would be my point of no return.

A VISITOR FROM MY PAST

All the same, the temptation seemed practically irresistible. Just when I was on the brink of disaster, however, a very special Someone paid me a visit and eased my tension. Jesus, my only true love, had come to see about me. Although it felt as if we had been apart for years, we picked up right where we had left off—in love. The truth is that He had never left me in the first place! It was I who had neglected the relationship. He had always been there. It was I who had been unfaithful, deserting Him to give my attention to natural affairs. He had never stopped loving me.

From the very beginning, I was the one who had not taken all of my troubles to Jesus or confided in Him my deepest emotions. Believing that I had failed Him, but thinking at the same time that I did not have to acknowledge Him when I felt my needs were being met, I had somehow been under the impression that I could love Him on my terms—in other words, conditionally. I had not realized that Jesus' love for me was unconditional, faithful, and everlasting. In response to His constant love, I needed to be faithful to Him as well.

Jesus understood my earthly situations and concerns. He just did not want me to be so preoccupied with natural events that I forgot spiritual affairs. Neither did He want me to try to handle my problems alone. I was simply to cast all my cares upon Him (1 Peter 5:7). My cares included my injured past, my disappointing marriage, my reckless insecurity, my unstable tendencies, and all my weaknesses.

Jesus visited me at the height of my temptation and dared me to resist Him. Beckoning me to confide in Him, He challenged me to love Him, not as I had before, but with a greater love—with all of my heart. As I knelt at His feet, He encouraged me to renew my vows of holy matrimony and rededicate myself in faithfulness, fidelity, chastity, loyalty, obedience, and service to Him for the rest of my life. I did—and He has taken care of the rest.

NEW BEGINNINGS

Today, my emotional affair has ended. Taking my faithful Friend, Jesus, with me, I initiated the painful but necessary breakup. It took time, love, and a lot of prayer, but the wounds from that fruitless relationship are now completely healed. Since I am in full, victorious recovery, the wounds from my past have begun to mend, as well, and my marriage has been restored. The man I am married to is the man whom I truly love. With love and God, there are no impossibilities, which is why Harry and I are both proud, happy parents now.

Last but not least, my relationship with Christ, my first love, is whole and entire. In Him, I want for nothing. We have a regular dialogue now, daily conversation that constantly energizes me. He is mine, and I am His, in both my times of need and my blessed seasons. I praise Him for His goodness to me and for His faithfulness. He has never cheated on me, nor will I ever again put another before Him. I have discovered that He is truly the world's greatest Lover.

Most of all, I am grateful that in the midst of the strongest temptation I have yet experienced, and in many troubled times since, Jesus has always come to my rescue and provided me a way of escape. I now know the exit door by heart: it is that comforting refuge within the safety of His loving, outstretched arms.

GOD'S ESCAPE ROUTE

[13] *No temptation has overtaken you except such as is common to man; but God is faithful, who will not allow you to be tempted beyond what you are able, but with the temptation will also make the way of escape, that you may be able to bear it.*
(1 Corinthians 10:13)

When we accept Jesus' death as complete payment for our sins and come into a right relationship with Him, our iniquities are forgiven, and our sins are no longer remembered (Jeremiah 31:34). However, we must keep in mind where we are vulnerable to the Enemy's enticements, since forgiveness does not guarantee that our flesh is always able to resist temptation as we ought to. Christ cautioned His disciples:

> [41] *Watch and pray, lest you enter into temptation. The spirit indeed is willing, but the flesh is weak.*
> (Matthew 26:41)

God already knows each and every area in which we can be tempted, but He has assured us that He will not allow us to undergo any temptation beyond what we are able to resist or beyond those things to which we are capable of saying no. God does not stop at this promise, however, but goes on to let us know that, just in case we become too weak and begin to feel that we cannot hold on and that our fall is inevitable, He will help us by providing a way of escape for us, through which we can successfully bypass Satan's lure. It is in these times that God makes for us a classic "way out of no way." Nevertheless, when He does provide the escape route, it is up to us to run toward the exit!

DENIAL AND DELIVERANCE

The apostle Paul also told us that being tempted is an experience that is *"common to man"* (1 Corinthians 10:13). Therefore, do not be alarmed when your own temptations and tests of faith come around!

> [12] *Beloved, do not think it strange concerning the fiery trial which is to try you, as though some strange thing happened to you;*
> [13] *but rejoice...also be glad with exceeding joy.*
> (1 Peter 4:12–13)

⁶ In this you greatly rejoice, though now for a little while, if need be, you have been grieved by various trials,
⁷ that the genuineness of your faith, being much more precious than gold that perishes, though it is tested by fire, may be found to praise, honor, and glory at the revelation of Jesus Christ.

(1 Peter 1:6–7)

Even in areas where you may have never thought you could be tempted, the Lord will often allow you to experience that temptation just to show you what deep, hidden darkness is really lurking inside of you. He, of course, already knows what is there. Sometimes, however, we can think that we are too spiritual to become ensnared, or we become so puffed up in our Christianity that we suppress through denial our innermost lusts. Rather than facing those desires and admitting that our flesh is corrupt, we often refuse to acknowledge that Christians still have carnal natures that are ever at war with our renewed spirits and minds. Instead, we need to admit the truth about our condition, along with the apostle Paul:

¹⁹ For the good that I will to do, I do not do; but the evil I will not to do, that I practice.
²⁰ Now if I do what I will not to do, it is no longer I who do it, but sin that dwells in me.
²¹ I find then a law, that evil is present with me, the one who wills to do good.
²² For I delight in the law of God according to the inward man.
²³ But I see another law in my members, warring against the law of my mind, and bringing me into captivity to the law of sin which is in my members.
²⁴ O wretched man that I am! Who will deliver me from this body of death?
²⁵ I thank God; through Jesus Christ our Lord! So then, with the mind I myself serve the law of God, but with the flesh the law of sin. (Romans 7:19–25)

True deliverance comes only through real honesty with God and trusting Him to deal with our sinful natures. If we have chosen to deny that our natural lusts exist, we may be totally caught off guard when these desires do finally push through and resurface in our lives. In our surprise and confusion, we can more easily get caught in the very snare that we had, in our denial, concealed behind the facade of piety.

When we finally learn to be completely truthful with ourselves and with the Lord by admitting that we have great weaknesses and vulnerabilities, especially in the area of relationships, then He can provide us with a way out of our fruitless liaisons. As we allow Him to heal our broken hearts and wounded spirits, our relationships will also become whole and healthy.

Part 4

Faulty Relationships:

When the Way I'm Loving You Is Wrong, but I Want to Love You Right

Faulty Relationships:

When the Way I'm Loving You Is Wrong, but I Want to Love You Right

*P*ossibly, you have already cleared out all of the former idols in your life, including those forbidden relationships that once attracted you so much. And, maybe, you are not even tempted anymore to become embroiled in some torrid but fruitless alliance. Your relationship problem may seem minor in comparison. Quite possibly, you are involved in an honorable, God-sanctioned union, but the connection with your partner seems to have soured. The warm intimacy you once shared has turned into cold detachment. Your marriage feels like it is on the rocks instead of being built on the Rock.

You may be feeling very stuck in a lousy situation and just have no idea what to do about it anymore. You

127

once promised before God to love, honor, and cherish your mate "until death do us part," and you have no intention of going back on your vow of lifelong fidelity, even if it kills you. But, if you are really honest, deep down inside lurks the nagging desire for a way out of this no-win situation in which you are trapped. You may have even secretly wished that your spouse would go out and commit adultery just so you would have biblical justification to file for divorce!

Hold on! Don't give up yet! There is a solution, other than a sin-ridden choice that could lead to even more disaster than you are in right now. I want to give you renewed hope that your heavenly Father will not leave you stranded in a loveless union, and so I am praying this for you:

> [13] *Now may the God of hope fill you with all joy and peace in believing, that you may abound in hope by the power of the Holy Spirit.* (Romans 15:13)

I know that just now your spouse may seem to be your enemy because you are at such odds with one another. Where once your home was peaceful and serene, it has become the battlefront for your personal war. However, God will meet you right in the midst of your intense conflict and negotiate a lasting peace, if you are willing to act according to His rules.

> [7] *When a man's ways please the LORD, He makes even his enemies to be at peace with him.* (Proverbs 16:7)

When you begin to act in faith and do what God wants you to do, He will step in and accomplish what you cannot. You may feel as if your marriage is impossible to heal, but our Lord is the God of the impossible. If He could reconcile the absolute hostility between the Jews and the Gentiles and unite them together through His

Son's death on the cross, I am certain that He is able to bring peace and wholeness to your fractionalized marriage. As you read the following Scripture passage, personalize it with your name and the name of your spouse, and accept it as a promise for the future of your marital relationship:

> [14] *For He Himself is our peace, who has made both [husband and wife] one, and has broken down the middle wall of separation,*
> [15] *having abolished in His flesh the enmity,...so as to create in Himself one new man [and union] from the two, thus making peace,*
> [16] *and that He might reconcile them both to God in one body through the cross, thereby putting to death the enmity.*
> [17] *And He came and preached peace to you who were afar off and to those who were near.*
> (Ephesians 2:14–17)

Read on, and learn some of the things you can do to fix your faltering relationship or simply to improve and fix up a slighty faulty one.

> [18] *If it is possible, as much as depends on you, live peaceably with all men.*   (Romans 12:18)

This includes your mate. Just keep in mind that God only requires that you do what you are capable of doing. He never asks you to do the impossible—that's His job.

9

Of Apples and Oranges

*I*ntegral to the process of perfecting our intimate relationships is a willingness on all of our parts to be open and honest about ourselves. As men and women, males and females, members of opposite sexes, two separate genders, we have to be truthful enough with ourselves to define, acknowledge, and know first who we are as individuals and then who we are as partners in our interplay with our respective mates. We need to know what our similarities are, what our differences are, and what are the ways in which we interact with one another.

We also need to fearlessly confront the issue of our sexuality. Sexuality is a God-given, positive facet of our human existence and experience. It is not something that will go away, even if we Christians determine that, personally, we are just too righteous or spiritual to candidly discuss the subject of sexuality. Only when God's people begin to shamelessly accept and seriously address who we are in entirety, fully embracing both our spiritual and natural realities, will we be able to learn the ways in which we can properly deal with and relate to one another as preordained, predetermined, and predesigned by our Creator.

> [7] *Wisdom is the principal thing; therefore get wisdom. And in all your getting, get understanding.*
>
> (Proverbs 4:7)

SEPARATE BUT EQUAL

In spite of what liberal laws, certain progressive movements, and some scientific studies tell us, we must first accept the obvious truth that men and women significantly differ in many respects. Unquestionably, we are very similar to one another, as well—mostly in a general human way. The fact remains, however, that males and females are separate, sometimes opposing, and often contrasting genders. As such, we have distinct behaviors, roles, responsibilities, and purposes, according to the original intention of God. God was the first one, in fact, to assign gender roles.

> [16] *To the woman He said: "I will greatly multiply your sorrow and your conception; in pain you shall bring forth children; your desire shall be for your husband, and he shall rule over you."*
> [17] *Then to Adam He said, "Because you have heeded the voice of your wife, and have eaten from the tree of which I commanded you, saying, 'You shall not eat of it': cursed is the ground for your sake; in toil you shall eat of it all the days of your life.*
> [18] *"Both thorns and thistles it shall bring forth for you, and you shall eat the herb of the field.*
> [19] *"In the sweat of your face you shall eat bread till you return to the ground, for out of it you were taken; for dust you are, and to dust you shall return."*
> (Genesis 3:16–19)

Of Apples and Oranges

Our differences as men and women, it seems, are the crux of the mystery of why we come together as naturally and easily as we do—when we do—in the first place.

> [18] *There be three things which are too wonderful for me, yea, four which I know not:*
> [19] *The way of an eagle in the air; the way of a serpent upon a rock; the way of a ship in the midst of the sea; and the way of a man with a maid.*
> (Proverbs 30:18–19 KJV)

Yet, even in our successful pairings, we are ever reminded of the distinctiveness of our gender perspectives. With all of the problems, discrepancies, and potent misunderstandings that inevitably surface between us, sometimes we become detached from the very people we once claimed to have loved so fiercely.

> [28] *But even if you do marry, you have not sinned; and if a virgin marries, she has not sinned. Nevertheless such will have trouble in the flesh, but I would spare you.* (1 Corinthians 7:28)

Before the predictable contrasts build to the point of becoming "irreconcilable differences" and permanently separate a God-fearing couple, an accurate assessment of gender roles and tendencies is needed. In an effort to clearly illustrate a few aspects of the differences between men and women, allow me to give the following analogy.

A FRUITFUL COMPARISON

Let us say that a man is an apple. A careful comparison to this fruit is one of the greatest ways to explain males. If you think about it, similar to a typical man, an apple boasts great things of itself on the outside: it is shiny, perhaps even a bit flashy with its vibrant color; it

133

is tough and smooth at the same time; and overall it looks good, even if it happens to have a few rough spots here and there. Of course, there are plenty of bad apples to be found, as well—apples that appear to be good for food but actually turn out to be full of empty holes, slimy worms, and rotting decay!

LAYERED FOR A REASON

Nevertheless, the quality of an apple's outer surface has a lot to do with its primary function. Covering the apple is the skin, which is most essential. Science tells us that the skin of an apple contains most of the vitamins and nutrients that make it healthy for the consumer. Nutrition, however, is not the entire purpose for the skin. The skin is actually on the apple to cover and protect the meat, or flesh, of the fruit.

The flesh of the apple provides nourishment. By it the thirst is quenched and the appetite satisfied. Even so, this is not the true purpose of the apple's flesh. The fact of the matter is that the meat of the apple is really there to cover the apple's core. And the core, which offers structure to the fruit, also has an underlying, more significant purpose: it houses the seed. So, the role of the skin is to cover the meat, the role of the meat is to cover the core, and the role of the core is to cover the seed.

Thus, a man is an apple in that the entire multi-layered quality of apples represents the main role and duty of males—to cover. In the eyes of God, the primary purpose of a man in a committed relationship is to provide a covering and protection for the woman in his life.

[23] *For the husband is head of the wife, as also Christ is head of the church; and He is the Savior of the body.* (Ephesians 5:23)

[3] *But I want you to know that the head of every man is Christ, the head of woman is man, and the head of Christ is God.* (1 Corinthians 11:3)

Of Apples and Oranges

FAILURE TO PROVIDE A COVERING

In Genesis, we find a scriptural account of what happens when a man fails to live up to the responsibility God has placed upon him. As you read this story, keep in mind that the God-ordained custom in those days was that when a man died, leaving his wife a childless widow, his brother was to marry the widow and sire a male heir, who could then inherit the dead man's share of the family fortunes and provide for his widowed mother.

[6] *Then Judah took a wife for Er his firstborn, and her name was Tamar.*

[7] *But Er, Judah's firstborn, was wicked in the sight of the LORD, and the LORD killed him.*

[8] *And Judah said to Onan, "Go in to your brother's wife and marry her, and raise up an heir to your brother."*

[9] *But Onan knew that the heir would not be his; and it came to pass, when he went in to his brother's wife, that he emitted on the ground, lest he should give an heir to his brother.*

[10] *And the thing which he did displeased the LORD; therefore He killed him also.*

[11] *Then Judah said to Tamar his daughter-in-law, "Remain a widow in your father's house till my son Shelah is grown." For he said, "Lest he also die like his brothers." And Tamar went and dwelt in her father's house.*

[12] *Now in the process of time the daughter of Shua, Judah's wife, died; and Judah was comforted, and went up to his sheepshearers at Timnah, he and his friend Hirah the Adullamite.*

[13] *And it was told Tamar, saying, "Look, your father-in-law is going up to Timnah to shear his sheep."*

[14] *So she took off her widow's garments, covered herself with a veil and wrapped herself, and sat in an open place which was on the way to Timnah; for she saw that Shelah was grown, and she was not given to him as a wife.*

¹⁵ When Judah saw her, he thought she was a harlot, because she had covered her face.

¹⁶ Then he turned to her by the way, and said, "Please let me come in to you"; for he did not know that she was his daughter-in-law. So she said, "What will you give me, that you may come in to me?"

¹⁷ And he said, "I will send a young goat from the flock." So she said, "Will you give me a pledge till you send it?"

¹⁸ Then he said, "What pledge shall I give you?" So she said, "Your signet and cord, and your staff that is in your hand." Then he gave them to her, and went in to her, and she conceived by him.

¹⁹ So she arose and went away, and laid aside her veil and put on the garments of her widowhood.

²⁰ And Judah sent the young goat by the hand of his friend the Adullamite, to receive his pledge from the woman's hand, but he did not find her.

²¹ Then he asked the men of that place, saying, "Where is the harlot who was openly by the roadside?" And they said, "There was no harlot in this place."

²² So he returned to Judah and said, "I cannot find her. Also, the men of the place said there was no harlot in this place."

²³ Then Judah said, "Let her take them for herself, lest we be shamed; for I sent this young goat and you have not found her."

²⁴ And it came to pass, about three months after, that Judah was told, saying, "Tamar your daughter-in-law has played the harlot; furthermore she is with child by harlotry." So Judah said, "Bring her out and let her be burned!"

²⁵ When she was brought out, she sent to her father-in-law, saying, "By the man to whom these belong, I am with child." And she said, "Please determine whose these are; the signet and cord, and staff."

²⁶ So Judah acknowledged them and said, "She has been more righteous than I, because I did not give her to Shelah my son." And he never knew her again.   (Genesis 38:6–26)

Of Apples and Oranges

Onan, whose name most fittingly means "my iniquity," selfishly chose to spill his seed on the ground instead of fathering an heir with Tamar, causing her to remain childless and without an inheritance. Thus, she had no permanent covering. God was angered at Onan's perversion, and like his brother before him, God slew Onan because of his wickedness. As the patriarch of the family, Judah was equally guilty for not attending to the necessary provision for Tamar.

The lesson of this story is this: when men are not real men, when they are not the covering for their wives that God intends them to be, they waste their seed and destroy their women.

THE SCENT OF ORANGE BLOSSOMS

Fruitfully speaking, if a man is an apple, then a woman is an orange. Pleasant to look at, sweet, and fragrant, the female orange is impressionable, tender, and soft to the touch in a way that the male apple is not. Like the apple, the orange also has skin, but unlike him, the rind of an orange is not where the majority of her vitamins and nutrients are found. In order to get to the goods of an orange, this fruit must first be peeled.

Before we start "peeling" the woman, however, there are a few things that must be pointed out about her. First, you cannot hold and touch the orange without picking up her scent. There is no way of escaping the fact that, if you touch her, you will smell like her. She simply has a way of rubbing off on you. And the more you touch her, stroke her, hold her, and caress her, the more she releases her scent. Tragically, too many men are locked into the scents of women who do not belong to them!

What are the things that cause a woman to release her scent? There are plenty of them. For example, when she is fulfilled, she releases a scent. The scent she releases says, "I have need of nothing." When she is of high

137

esteem, she releases a scent. The scent she releases says, "I am a woman of virtue and worth." When she is held and caressed, she releases a scent. The scent she releases says, "I am loved." Indeed, men are motivated by and seek after the scents of women, but if a man mishandles his woman, she releases an acidic, neutralizing aroma that says, "Get away from me, you skunk!"

GETTING TO THE HEART OF THE MATTER

While the orange is being stroked and handled on the outside and her scent is filtering into the atmosphere, her juices are flowing and being stirred on the inside. The way to get to these juices, and the entire depth and substance of the woman, is to peel her. Before you get the wrong idea, undressing her is not what I am referring to at all. In fact, that will just cause her to try to cover herself up tightly and hide her real self from you.

Conversation is one of the primary tools that peel a woman. A woman can meet a man and consider him desirable because he has a decent job, drives a nice car, or is good-looking. However, if the woman herself has any depth at all, she will soon tire of that man if he cannot converse or freely communicate with her!

Through a man's conversation with her, a woman will begin to reveal secrets and truths about herself. The process of pulling back the peel of a choice orange is not always easy. It takes time to peel a good woman. In fact, if you peel her too fast, she will probably sting you with her acidic juices! On the other hand, if you talk to her openly and honestly, encourage her with your understanding, and knead her gently, it will not be long before you get to see just what mysteries lie beneath her pretty surface.

Once the orange has been peeled, you do have the option of simply going ahead and devouring it—except that in doing so, you would be making a grave mistake. Another thin layer on the surface of the orange must be removed in order to get down to the bare emotions of the woman being dealt with. It is at this point in the peeling process that a man begins to touch the center, or heart, of his orange. At the pulling back of that last, lingering film of skin, a man begins to uncover his lady's hurts and pains—the unsightly deep bruises from past relationships, the natural defenses and guardedness she has constructed as protective measures against the storms of life, and the scars from fateful advances and seductions of men who meant her no good!

A female is amazing, yet at the same time, she is a maze. Be warned, then, that she is not as easily exited as she is entered! This means that a man ought to proceed with carefulness, caution, and certainty when lifting that final, ultrafine layer.

When peeling your women, men, you want to speak lovingly to them, assuring them that you will not take them through the same treacherous routes of romance that other men have. Not only that, but it also is imperative that you take your time, after having completed the peeling process, to do some serious cutting away of the waste that previous forbidden fruits in your lady's life have left behind. Don't be in such a hurry to consume your orange that you forget to clean out the lingering residue of the other men who got to her before you came along. Without a doubt, you want your woman to know that you will love her, provide for her, and treat her with the adoration and respect that the others could not or would not provide.

CAUTION: HANDLE WITH CARE

The sad, unfortunate reality is that too many women in Christianity (not to mention those abiding outside of Christ) have been emotionally raped by the various men in their lives. Hurriedly peeled and eaten too soon, these women were plucked from the trees of their potential and destiny while they were not yet ripe.

On the other hand, if they were ready to be picked, more often than not the men who chose them did not know how to select the proper orange to fit their own tastes, or they did not know how to properly love and appreciate the orange's fruit. Insensitive, inexperienced, and unskilled, these men removed the delicate skins of their women, opened them up, and exploited their innocence and tenderness. In doing so, they tore their flesh. Instead of respecting and enjoying their female fruits with reserve, they greedily, selfishly ravished them! They devoured the flesh of their oranges with the boorishness of a barbarian instead of savoring their oranges' tastes and textures and aromas with the sensitivity of a gourmet.

STRUCTURAL DIFFERENCES

Once a man has peeled back that final layer of his lady, nevertheless, if he is not in too much of a hurry to consume her, he will notice that there is a slight doorway by which he can actually open her up. And once he has exposed her center, he will see that there are several sections to his woman. The orange is not like the apple, who is only one piece; she has several divisions or compartments. If a woman is to become his, a man must go through the process of picking her off the tree, cleaning her up, peeling her outer skin, peeling her inner skin, getting rid of the residue below her skin, and opening up all of the sections within her. Only after this extremely intense process and careful handling will he be able to experience and know his orange fully, and become a significant, inseparable part of her.

Speaking of the apple, when you deal with a man, ladies, realize that there is no way in the world for you to peel him—certainly not with your hands, anyway. The only way to get on the inside of an apple is to bite him or cut him somehow! But notice that when you do cut into the apple, he has no sections. You find only layers of flesh, core, and seeds.

It is important to note that the apple's particular constitution makes it relatively easy for an insect of some sort to enter him while he is not yet ripe and to actually feed on his flesh until he is consumed from the inside out! So, ladies, to get to know your apple you have to go through the process of assessing his exterior, selecting him, and bringing him home to become a part of your life. Then, when you finally get around to biting into him or cutting him open, you just may discover that he is only a shell of attractiveness. What appeared to be delectable on the outside may prove to be only skin-deep, because on the inside, he may be nothing but worms and rottenness!

A female is not like this, however. There simply is no way that a worm can live inside of her. She has acidic chemicals from her extrinsic rind to her private center that burn and consume any infectious material that may try to enter and contaminate her. Even when the men of her past have wounded, scarred, and left her with their filthy residue, she is often yet salvageable. There is usually some bit of sweetness to be found somewhere in her.

INHERENT REGENERATIVE ABILITIES

Within the various sections of a woman lies her salvation from total spoilage. These multiple segments demonstrate the female's emotional complexity and represent different aspects of her resilience. For example, in one of her sections, there might be love; in another, joy; in still others, there might be patience, faith, understanding, and trust. The number of segments within a given orange varies from fruit to fruit: some have six sections, others might have eight, and still others may have ten or twelve divisions.

However, in each individual section of the orange, in each separate compartment of her emotional makeup, seeds are found. The purpose of these seeds is to grow as replacements for whatever parts of her have been lost or have run dry, due to the negative effects of the unfruitful relationships she may become involved in. Amazingly, God has equipped the woman with multiple seeds in her various compartments so that she might regenerate and get back what the various hard, bitter, rotten apples in her life have stolen from her!

When investigating the emotional sections of a woman, one finds that the number of seeds in each compartment varies. In one section, there may be two, three, or four seeds. Then, in another section, there may be no seeds at all. Each segment bears its own special seeds, and the number of seeds contained within each section is based upon the foreknowledge and design of God concerning each individual woman.

The Lord knew before you were even born, ladies, that you would have to go through the various trials of relationships—some of you, one, two, three, or more times before meeting your Mr. Right. Similar to a cat with nine lives, God decided to give you what was necessary for you to retrieve, time and time again, the womanly gifts, traits, and attributes that have been unfairly, undeservingly taken from you. The corrupt apples of your past involvements or the general detriment of your less-than-ideal romantic relationships may have temporarily stolen from you, but God has promised:

[25] *I will restore to you the years that the swarming locust has eaten, the crawling locust, the consuming locust, and the chewing locust.* (Joel 2:25)

[11] *For I know the thoughts that I think toward you, says the LORD, thoughts of peace and not of evil, to give you a future and a hope.* (Jeremiah 29:11)

In His infinite wisdom, God predesigned you women with the inherent powers to recover from the damage caused by all the different, nasty insects He knew would be in your lives. He even foresaw every type of rascal who would try to strip you naked and devour you, but He planted within you the seeds of restoration long before you actually needed them.

THE MULTIFACETED TAMAR

Tamar, the resilient woman of Scripture mentioned earlier, is an exceptional example of the female's natural regenerative quality. Taking the desperate measure of prostitution in order to secure herself economically, Tamar was a woman of decency who was brought low by an indecent man. Onan, who failed to fulfill his masculine obligation toward his wife by refusing to impregnate her, left Tamar uncovered, which meant that she was exposed, vulnerable, and forced to fend for herself in a Hebrew society that favored men. Tamar found redemption in the end, nevertheless, after making the controversial decision to "play the harlot"; her determination to have male protection did finally bring to her what was her natural entitlement as a woman: a child and a covering.

Without a doubt, Tamar was a select orange, containing multiple sections—some of which were fortitude, faith, and adaptability—and possessing many seeds of resourcefulness. Her story of perseverance and ultimate victory proves to us that the true essence and beauty of a woman is revealed when she makes up her mind that in spite of the wreckage and damage inflicted upon her by the abusive, irresponsible, and undutiful men in her life, she will not give up and die. Tamar's personal creed, as well as that of the majority of the world's strong Christian women, must have been along the lyrical lines of the popular 1970s tune, "I Will Survive."

THE CARE AND PRUNING OF APPLE TREES

Women are not the only halves of romantic relationships who sometimes need extra attention and caretaking, however. Indeed, it is often the case that a relatively good man will require the specialized love, patience, and attention of his wife so that the ragged, imperfect, unpolished areas of his flawed character might be pruned from him. This qualifies him as a diamond-in-the-rough—or better still, as a potential-laden tree, which needs individualized pruning so that it might begin to bear healthy, desirable fruit!

> [6] [Jesus] *also spoke this parable: "A certain man had a fig tree planted in his vineyard, and he came seeking fruit on it and found none.*
> [7] *"Then he said to the keeper of his vineyard, 'Look, for three years I have come seeking fruit on this fig tree and find none. Cut it down; why does it use up the ground?'*
> [8] *"But he answered and said to him, 'Sir, let it alone this year also, until I dig around it and fertilize it.*
> [9] *"'And if it bears fruit, well. But if not, after that you can cut it down.'"* (Luke 13:6–9)

Using this parable to further illustrate our point, we could say that the unproductive, displeasing tree represents a man who is not properly exercising his duty toward women and is thus barren in the context of relationships. And if a man is a tree, the earth in which he is planted and the soil from which he receives nourishment for growth are analogous to the home environment created by the women with whom he has been in relationship.

When men are involved in multiple relationships, they are grown in the fields of different women. As a result, when they do finally find their permanent mates, they are often not totally what their wives need and desire. When a man comes from the unhealthy, lacking, or stripped soil of another female, a woman sometimes has to replant her man in her own soil and fertilize him with the nutrients and minerals of her particular choosing, because he is now hers.

In this parable, the man is the fig tree that needs to be dug out of its corrupt soil of the past, fertilized, and given the proper growth supplements after replanting. The "owner" who complains about the barren tree and demands that it be cut down is often the man's mother-in-law or another caring individual who opposes the negligence of the husband toward his wife. It follows, then, that this wife is none other than the compassionate, forgiving keeper of the vineyard.

As the keeper defends the undesirable tree before its owner, so a woman, when she feels that her currently bad relationship might actually be salvageable, sometimes has to confront her mother, father, family members, friends, and other onlookers with a certain declaration that she will stand by, support, and nurture her man until she herself comes to the realization that he is not worth her effort. In the meantime, however, she will take on the challenging role of becoming his loyal, faithful caretaker.

The fact of the matter is that, sometimes, when a man appears to be absolutely rotten, he actually has great potential to become very good. A corrupt product of his corrupt environment, sometimes a man who is bad is really not so bad that he has to be permanently discarded or thrown away.

Revisiting the first analogy of a man being an apple, some men are fruits who have only spots of decay; they are not actually rotten to the core. If the undesirable aspects of their personalities, attitudes, and behaviors were to be carefully cut away and discarded by females who recognized their promise, they would turn out to be truly healthy and pleasant for consumption. At the same time, in viewing men as trees, if the crooked, immature, diseased, or unyielding ones are nurtured by women who really care, and they are replanted in richer soil, the fruit they will yield might be surprisingly good and satisfying.

The woman, being the caring keeper of the vineyard, has compassion on this less-than-ideal tree who is her man. She understands that the fig tree is actually a desert plant that, having been planted in the strange environment of a vineyard, has been situated in a foreign climate and soil conditions. She realizes that this is quite possibly the reason why the tree will not produce. So, in the face of its detractors, she stands up for the tree. She determines to dig her man up from the corrupt soil of his former girlfriends, pull up his shallow roots, eliminate the corruption and improper influences of his former environment, fertilize him with her undying love and devotion, shelter him through the storms and inclement weather of life, nurture him with her faith and support, stick with him through the trials and tests of the relationship, believe in him amid all the turbulence, stabilize him with the restrictive guide-wires of her personal standards, and nurse him back to emotional and psychological health.

After all of the keeping, dressing, and caretaking she can summon, if he still fails to produce and has not become a reputable, decent man who provides a proper covering for her, then she will cut him down. Either by allowing him to leave or by removing herself from the relationship, this unquestionably tired woman will finally be rid of her unredeemable tree!

PERSONALIZED GROOMING

In all honesty, I myself, like a great majority of men, entered my marriage relationship already grown in other women's fields and vineyards. Involved in several relationships before I met my wife, I developed little responsibility or respectfulness toward females because none of the women I had dealings with after reaching adulthood had required that of me. Unfortunately, the various soils of these women failed to foster any type of personal, positive growth or relationship etiquette in me.

146

So, by the time I met my life-partner, I was a severely bent, twisted, crooked little tree! This meant that my wife could choose either to consume my corrupt fruit and suffer the inevitable consequences—spiritual canker sores, indigestion, diarrhea, and ulcers—that such tainted food would cause, or she could replant my tree and cultivate the type of fruit she desired.

It is still somewhat difficult for me to accept sometimes, but I was the product of a family environment that was indisputably, entirely dysfunctional. Specifically, my father had been a woman beater. Since I had been a witness to and the target of his abuse, I was generationally cursed with his violent tendencies. His behavior toward women was not something that revealed itself in me, his impressionable son, immediately. For years, an emotional rage and desire to batter lay dormant in me, but it wasn't until I had been married for three whole years that the sleeping dog awakened.

It was during one particularly heated argument between my wife and me that I unwisely determined that, in order to get my point across to her, I had to physically drive it home. Immediately, the quiet, gentle woman to whom I was wed was forced to adapt her meek personality to that of the angry authoritarian before her. She had to swing the ax of her hot displeasure powerfully against my disrespectful, presumptuous, tree trunk and cut me down to proper size. I humbly admit that ever since my spouse's rather violent uprooting of my tree from the depleted dirt in which I had previously lived, I have happily and healthily been replanted, fertilized, grown, and groomed in a new brand of soil—her own! And the truth is that I wouldn't have it any other way. Let me tell you the story.

CUT DOWN TO SIZE

Times were tough back in the days when I first began circuit preaching and evangelizing. Delightfully wedded for three years to a wonderful lady, we had two equally wonderful children to care for—except that money was extremely tight. Under those circumstances, the eighteen hundred dollars that I received during one particular ministry crusade meant a whole lot to me, because I considered it to be a whole lot of dough! Happy to finally be making a significant contribution to my family and household, I forwarded the money home to my wife. Soon afterward, I returned home with even more cash in my pocket. This I had intended to add to the funds I had already sent home—funds that I expected to be there when I arrived!

Little did I realize that one doesn't always get what he wishes for. I greeted my wife upon reaching home, genuinely glad to see her. Once we had exchanged our loving pleasantries, nevertheless, my conversation quickly went to the subject of the cash.

"Where's the money, baby?" I asked sweetly. But my wife continued to inquire about my welfare.

"How are you doing?" she wanted to know, not yet ready to address the important issue.

Again I asked, "Where's the money, baby?"

After a considerably long pause, my wife replied calmly, "I spent it."

"You what?" I asked incredulously, not wanting to believe the truth of what I had just heard. I prayed that my ears were deceiving me. "You did what?"

Growing defensive, the woman whom I had always known as quiet and subdued, angrily shouted, "I spent it!"

In response, I became quiet and grew silently furious, as the demons of rage awakened and began to rise up within me. My mind raced: "She spent the money? How could she?" More than anything, I wanted to strike out at something, and my wife was the obvious target. I needed to lay hands on the sick, so that she would re-cover!

Back and forth we argued, yelling at the top of our lungs. Full of rage, my back leg braced; my hand dropped down; my palm was shaking at my side. I said to myself, "I'm going to anoint her good!" Drawing my hand back, my arm moved in what seemed like slow-motion incre-ments, making me feel like the Bionic Man. But my wife became the Bionic Woman, and in similar slow motion, she raised her arm in an effort to block my forceful blow.

I had been going for her face, but instead, I caught her whole arm. When my hand landed upon her flesh, the hit was so hard, it left my own palm stinging. The slap was so powerful, in fact, that if I had struck her face as intended, I would have taken off her entire head!

My wife ran out of the room screaming! I stood in front of the television, flipping the channels with the remote, and yelled out, "I bet you won't spend any more money in this house!"

All of a sudden, I heard a great ruckus coming from the direction of the kitchen. My wife was still some-where, screaming shrilly, "Nobody puts his hands on me! You don't have any business hitting me! Even my own father didn't hit me!"

Still in front of the TV, I yelled, "Shut up that noise in there! I'm the authority in this house…"

But before I could get it all out, she came back into the den, and somebody turned out the lights. This tiny woman had hit me on my head with a big, black iron skillet! Before I could finish counting the tiny stars that began to dance before my blurring vision, I was flat on my back. I looked up and saw Abraham, Isaac, and Jacob. I wanted to see Jesus, the One who died for me!

My wife stood over me with the frying pan in her hand, swinging it from side to side. The prophetic anointing suddenly fell upon her, and she begin to speak into my life as I lay on the floor of the den, still down for the count! I was nearly raptured at that point, but my wife called my spirit back into my body. Looking down at me, she declared, "I love you, darling, but thus says the Lord: 'If you ever put your hands on her again, I will kill you!'"

Peering up at my wife through glazed eyes, all I could say was "Yes, Lord!"

It took me quite a while to get up from my place on the altar of the den floor, but when I did, I was a changed man. I had a newfound respect and admiration for the courageous, beautiful woman I had married. And yet, I wouldn't recommend hitting someone with an iron skillet—you could seriously injure someone that way.

HANDLING CONFLICT GOD'S WAY

Now when my wife and I get into arguments, we do only that—argue. There is absolutely no hitting or physical force involved. As all of us who are married can attest, arguments, disputes, and fussings are inevitable between mates. If there is absolutely no conflict in a marriage, one of the partners is just a shadow of the other and is, therefore, rather dull.

[17] *As iron sharpens iron, so a man sharpens the countenance of his friend.* (Proverbs 27:17)

Personally, I view conflict as an almost necessary part of the bonding process between couples, as it truly tests the durability of the union that, hopefully, God has put together. At least for my wife and myself—two people who are crazy about each other, but who are also at times driven crazy by one another—working through the past conflicts and problems in our relationship has ensured our preservation and permanence as a loving, committed couple.

At the same time, I now realize that spankings, whippings, and corporal punishment are exclusively for the correction of children. In effect, it took just one blow for me to truly know! I thank my wife for teaching me the invaluable lesson of uncompromising respect for her, and for all women. I am truly grateful to her for loving me enough not to discard my bent, obnoxious tree, but rather to grow me in her rich, abundant soil, saturated with patience, understanding, and humble submission.

Indeed, it is my wife who has wisely set the precedent in our marriage that says physical contact with one another can only be motivated by love. Now, not only do I respect this woman, but I fully admire, appreciate, and adore her. I am willing to work out our problems through honest conversation with her, no matter how heated our "discussions" may become when we are each striving to convince the other of the rightness of our own viewpoint.

And I trust that, by now, at least some of my points of view have made an impression on you. May God sweetly bless and restore the healthy companionship between you and the significant other in your life.

10

Marriage Matters

*I*mpaired marriages can be a generational trend, resulting from faulty modeling. What children see acted out in front of them in their homes and what they are taught—the subliminal and blatant messages that are passed down to them—can affect their future relationships as well as their personalities.

For example, females are traditionally taught to be sweet, loving, and compassionate. From birth, their lives are permeated with this tenderness of heart and spirit: from the soft pastel colors of their clothing, the lace that lines their cribs, and the cuddling they receive and are encouraged to reciprocate, young women are nurtured to be nurturers. By the time a girl is a year old, she has been given her first baby doll, with which she practices her mothering skills. By the age of three, she receives a Barbie doll, which sends an equally feminine though somewhat different message, making her subconsciously aware of her womanhood and sexuality.

The toy industry and its manufacturers shoulder a great part of the responsibility for fostering the materialistic attitude that is evident in our society's young women. Greed and selfish acquisition are promoted by the luxury vehicles Barbie drives, the posh townhouses she owns, and her limitless wardrobe. Barbie and her boyfriend Ken, even though they are just dolls, model equally poor moral standards for girls by their jet-set lifestyles and living together outside of marriage. In addition, Barbie's multiple careers and entrepreneurial endeavors as teacher, astronaut, nurse, boutique owner, and much more—all of which she achieved without effort, education, or self-discipline—send an unhealthy message of the ease of total independence from outside sources, including men and God.

On the other hand, young boys are given trucks, baseball bats, jerseys, footballs, hockey pucks, and GI Joe dolls, all of which help to shape and reinforce their masculinity. Even beyond masculinity, young boys are taught the art of being macho—they are to be men who dominate. Boys learn early that it is manly to conquer and control whatever is immediately at hand, without considering the consequences, and to win at all costs.

Thus, the behaviors and attitudes a young man is taught are the direct opposites of those taught to a young woman. He is rough, while she is soft. Where she cuddles, he wrestles. She is taught to consider her future, while he learns to think in terms of the present. Where verbal expression and communication are concerned, the girl is encouraged to become extroverted, and the boy, more introverted.

OPPOSITES ATTRACT

One can see that if two people with these emotional, behavioral, and psychological extremes were to unite in marriage, the entire picture would be wrong. For example, in the neighborhood where I grew up, a young woman gave birth to a baby girl. By the time this baby girl was nine months old, her mother was pregnant again. This second baby, also a girl, was born when the first girl was only eighteen months old. An additional nine months later, the young woman became pregnant again. By the birth of the third baby, the oldest child was only twenty-seven months old, but she was needed by Mom for assistance with the new infant. So, the young mother sat her oldest child on the sofa, handed her the newborn baby (propped up with a pillow for support), and had the twenty-seven-month-old toddler feed her youngest sibling. Hence, the oldest daughter received her instructions in motherhood hardly before beginning the experience of childhood.

Understandably, by the time this oldest child was barely eighteen, she was ready to leave her mother's household and find a man to care for her. Soon after, she met a young man her age who was the youngest child in his family. As such, the idea and expectation that he himself was always to be cared for and catered to was inbred in the young man's nature and character, because his particular birth order had made him accustomed to being doted on. The two young people decided to come together, both secretly hoping to get their needs met through the other. However, because these two immature eighteen-year-olds were seeking the same things from each other—care and provisions—their union was troubled and unbalanced, since both wanted to receive and neither was truly capable of giving.

THE YOKE OF RELATIONSHIPS

The Scripture says, *"Do not be unequally yoked together with unbelievers"* (2 Corinthians 6:14). Unfortunately, when reading this Scripture, we tend to focus on the word *"unbelievers."* The fact of the matter is that you may both be believers, yet still be *"unequally yoked."* Let me clarify what the yoke means with an illustration.

A farmer selects two oxen as he prepares to plow his field. Placing a yoke on them, he fastens it and signals them to plow. After plowing half of his field, the farmer stops for a rest, returning to his porch. While having lemonade, he sees that the newly plowed rows are crooked, some of the lines running into each other. As he ponders this situation, he realizes that the yoke must not be designed to balance the relative strengths of the oxen. This imbalance caused the plowed lines to crash, making it impossible to plant seed or to reap a good harvest later.

POTENTIAL HINDRANCES TO A BALANCED MARRIAGE

Just as the farmer's yoke was not properly constructed to distribute the workload between the two animals, given the individual strengths and weaknesses of each, so the yoke of the marriage bond can develop in such a way as to distort the balance of power between husband and wife. I have observed over the years that certain dysfunctional behavioral patterns can form between husbands and wives that hinder the growth of their intimacy and prevent their production of good fruit.

1. Too Much or Not Enough Communication

When one member of a couple talks too much or when a spouse does not talk enough, the wrong messages are inevitably sent. In the former case, when the communication is excessive, it is quite often the female doing the talking, sometimes giving her husband the impression that she is a "know-it-all." Eventually, his tendency will be to tune out all her chatter because he thinks none of it has any relevance. On the other hand, when a husband tends to withhold communication and conversation, his wife interprets his silence as evidence of a "problem" that he doesn't want to talk about.

Men must understand that women tend to have a reservoir of emotions and experiences from their past, which they draw from for the present. Similar to the ebb

and flow of water, women are known to generate and regenerate communication. Husbands must be careful not
to fault their wives for their constant communicating; it
is their nature. At the same time, men can learn to be
more expressive and verbal, especially when there is a
serious need for discussion. However, the intelligent
woman who understands that the man's natural tendency is to be reserved in conversation will not attempt
to push him out of character by insisting that he "just
talk about it."

2. Confessing Your Past to Your Mate

When confession of past sins is being made, it is
important that the right individual hear the disclosure.
This is not always your spouse, even when the confession
concerns your relationship. Remember, issues of the past
that have already been confessed to God and covered by
the blood of Jesus do not necessarily need to be retrieved
from the Sea of Forgetfulness and shared with your
mate! Sometimes, your spouse is not prepared to hear
the whole, unvarnished truth about your past.

Many successful marriages have been destroyed
through the encouragement of spiritual leaders and others who promote untimely disclosure. I happen to know
of a particular marriage that crumbled, even though the
couple was at the peak of marital happiness, because a
traveling minister strongly encouraged the seminar attendees to "confess all" to their mates. Upon hearing this
advice, the husband revealed to his wife that he had engaged in an affair many years previously, while she was
pregnant with their first child. His wife was absolutely
brokenhearted and devastated by his admission, to the
extent that she could no longer continue in the marriage.
Indeed, having the affair was absolutely wrong on the
husband's part. However, had this man admitted his sin
and truly repented only to God, accepted the Lord's forgiveness and cleansing, and not heeded such unspiritual

advice, this once happy couple might still be married today.

If this man had felt the need to confess to someone, his best option would have been to seek out counseling with his pastor or another mature, trustworthy, spiritual leader in his own church. In doing so, he would have established an ongoing relationship with another man who could have guided him wisely, based on personal knowledge of the whole situation, and who could have held him accountable for his subsequent behavior.

Be mindful, dear reader, that in saying this, I am not advocating dishonesty or concealment. Rather, I am recommending that you use prudence when sharing the unseemly things of your past with your spouse. You need to know both your mate and the nature of your relationship so well that you can determine whether confession will indeed end up being good for your soul.

3. Comparing Your Mate with Others

If you like the idea of continually being in hot water with your mate, just make this a regular habit. Almost universally, women seem to be highly offended by this tendency in their men. Gentlemen, do not compare your wife with or to another woman. She wants you to be in love with her own unique qualities and individuality, not how she stacks up next to someone else, or even how something about her reminds you of another woman. She prides herself on being a Designer Original, so treat her as such. Ladies, the same is true concerning your husbands. Do not compare your mate with a previous man in your life—unless, of course, you are telling him how much better he is!

4. Dwelling on Your Partner's Weaknesses

For most of us, our sensitive spots are closely tied to our weaknesses. Pointing out another's faults and flaws not only produces hurt feelings, but it also makes you appear insensitive and arrogant, even if your only intention is to help. Getting others to address what you see as their shortcomings requires a delicate touch.

> [15] *But speaking the truth in love, we are to grow up in all aspects into Him, who is the head, even Christ.* (Ephesians 4:15 NAS)

Self-esteem, self-worth, and personal security are all built up and strengthened by emphasizing a person's positive characteristics. Dwelling on the individual's negative attributes can tear the positive ones down.

> [19] *Therefore let us pursue the things which make for peace and the things by which one may edify* [or, build up] *another.* (Romans 14:19)

> [11] *Therefore encourage one another, and build up one another....*
> [13] *Esteem them very highly in love....Live in peace with one another.* (1 Thessalonians 5:11, 13 NAS)

In summary, the philosophy that says showing others their weaknesses makes them stronger is, more often than not, false. Emphasis on weaknesses makes one weaker, is not encouraging, and definitely does not build the other up. Since the marriage relationship is about strengthening and esteeming our mates, we should focus on the positive aspects of our partners to help make them stronger.

5. Allowing Outsiders to Meddle in the Marriage

The Bible tells us, *"What God has joined together, let not man separate"* (Mark 10:9). Here, God is speaking about the actual institution of marriage as a covenant to be respected by those inside and outside of it. The marriage is set apart unto itself as a separate unit with its own identity. It does not include parents, children, friends, or even church leaders. Manipulation of the marital relationship by anyone outside of the union must not be tolerated, even if it comes from a well-meaning pastor or Christian counselor.

6. Clinging to Your Parents Instead of Your Spouse

[24] *Therefore shall a man leave his father and his mother, and shall cleave unto his wife: and they shall be one flesh.* (Genesis 2:24 KJV)

Parents often remain tied to their married children through an emotional umbilical cord long after the physical one has been cut. Parents' unsolicited involvement in their married children's lives is a subtle form of witchcraft, which needs to be broken through the power of the blood of Jesus.

On the other hand, adult children have often not grown up emotionally and financially and declared their independence from Mom and Dad by assuming the full responsibilities of adulthood. Frequently, it has been too easy for some to remain dependent on their parents rather than take on the burdens of supporting and making decisions for themselves. Such juvenile adults, however, pay a high price for remaining dependent: they have to surrender much of the control of their lives to their parents. When people like this get married, inevitably their opposite-sex parent has more influence over them than their mate does. This causes friction in the marriage because it injures the spouse's place as mate.

7. Sharing Intimate Information with Outsiders

We must be extremely careful of what we share about our marriages with people outside of our unions. Not only are the intimate details of our particular bonds none of their business, but quite often we are first turning to outside friends for consolation and support when we should be addressing any problem situations with our mates. Wives are often more guilty of actually committing this offense, but husbands share part of the responsibility when they fail to keep the lines of communication open or really listen to what their wives say.

8. Apologizing Later instead of First Getting Permission

The false assumption that sacrifice afterward is better than consideration and obedience in the first place (1 Samuel 15:22) is the basic fallacy behind a major problem in all too many marriages today. This hindrance creates very serious strife in a marriage—not *may* create or *possibly* creates or *might* create, but *absolutely* creates division! Too many husbands have the idea that they can do exactly what they want to do whenever they want to do it, as long as later, when the time of reckoning comes, they buy their wives dinner or a dress or produce some other type of bribe to make peace. However, the end result is quite tragic, when that "last straw" act of the husband occurs and breaks his wife's patience and spirit! Unknown to the man, the woman has in her storehouse of memories his track record of offenses. When she is finally destroyed by his last affront to her dignity, she will realize that all his former apologies—and gifts!—were insincere.

The moral of the story, then, is get permission, or it will cost you the money in your pocket and the peace in your relationship!

9. Projecting a False Character

Unfortunately, in many cases, the church has forced us as Christians to try to be who we are not. "Spiritual cloning" happens when a leading figure from the outside or a dominating personality within a church attracts others through charisma, authority, or allure. When weaker personalities attempt to mimic the outstanding person, they lose their own individuality and uniqueness. Taking on that person's character traits and personality, these envious people start to dress like, think like, talk like, worship like, laugh like, and even take on the peculiar mannerisms of the dominant personality. Of course, they carry home this facade, projecting a false character to their mates.

Institutions and industries other than the church that produce clones include the media, fashion, and Wall Street (the rat race). In times of crisis, however, when the storms of life are raging within relationships, the false character never fails to drop off, revealing the true individual behind the facade. This explosive situation has the potential of sparking disaster. Remember, who you are in the midst of the storm is who you really are.

10. Making Your Children the Focus of the Marriage

Again, it is necessary to emphasize that children are a part of the family, but not a part of the marriage. Because a mother is generally the main source of care and nurturance for her children, especially the younger and more dependent they are on her, she is particularly prone to neglecting her husband while tending to the offspring. She will often forego her first duty to the marriage and the meeting her husband's needs for their sakes. However, since the marital union was hopefully established before the children came along, her husband has proprietary rights to her focus and attention. When a woman allows her children to take up all of her time and energy, they usurp her husband's rightful place with her.

Therefore, we must be careful that our children do not manipulate our marriage bonds. To prevent it from happening, make decisions together, and stick to them—no matter how upset the kids may become.

REPLACEMENT THERAPY

Although the above list of faulty behaviors is by no means all-inclusive, the avoidance of these hindrances alone could go a long way to strengthen your marriage. However, when we humans try to change our behavior and we stop doing something we know is detrimental for us, we are predisposed to replace one bad habit with another. I suggest that in your attempts to fix the flaws in your marriage, you substitute God's design and follow His instructions for positive marital behavior:

> [21] *Submitting to one another in the fear of God.*
> [22] *Wives, submit to your own husbands, as to the Lord.*
> [23] *For the husband is head of the wife, as also Christ is head of the church; and He is the Savior of the body.*
> [24] *Therefore, just as the church is subject to Christ, so let the wives be to their own husbands in everything.*
> [25] *Husbands, love your wives, just as Christ also loved the church and gave Himself for her,*
> [26] *that He might sanctify and cleanse her with the washing of water by the word,*
> [27] *that He might present her to Himself a glorious church, not having spot or wrinkle or any such thing, but that she should be holy and without blemish.*
> [28] *So husbands ought to love their own wives as their own bodies; he who loves his wife loves himself.*
> [29] *For no one ever hated his own flesh, but nourishes and cherishes it, just as the Lord does the church.*
> [30] *For we are members of His body, of His flesh and of His bones.*
> [31] *"For this reason a man shall leave his father and mother and be joined to his wife, and the two shall become one flesh."*
> [33] *Nevertheless let each one of you in particular so love his own wife as himself, and let the wife see that she respects her husband.* (Ephesians 5:21–31, 33)

What a formula for a successful marriage!

Part 5

Fabulous Relationships:

When Loving You Is Right, and All's Right with the World

Fabulous Relationships:

When Loving You Is Right, and All's Right with the World

We all long to have the special kind of relationship with another human being in which we truly know and are known by each other. We desire that this knowledge be intimate, perceptive, total, and complete—a deep heart knowledge. We desperately want to be accepted, loved, and cherished for who we really are, in spite of our flaws and imperfections. Built into the human condition is a longing not to have to play games by pretending to be someone we are not; we want to be able to be authentic with at least one other person and still be loved. Moreover, our Mr. Goodbars and Ms. Rights are our perfect counterparts who do love and accept us unselfishly and eternally.

That concept, with slight personal variations, is the essence of the image of the ideal relationship we each carry deep inside. As I have stated previously, we have been designed by God to be relational beings. Thus, the need for intimacy is woven into the fabric of our lives and will not disappear by praying it away or by willing it to leave or by ignoring it. Each of us must come to terms with this aspect of life and with how to legitimately meet this burning desire for relational fulfillment, no matter what our marital status may be.

Most of us define fabulous relationships in terms of knowing and being known, accepting and being accepted, loving and being loved, while often emphasizing such additional components as commitment, communication, romance, and chemistry. Yet, in our attempts to find and establish our dream friendships and unions, we have taken forbidden, fruitless side trails that lead to dead ends instead of staying on the path that *"leads to life"* (Matthew 7:14), which God has specifically planned for each one of us.

Usually, we have gone off in the opposite direction from the way God wants us to travel as we try to fill the aching void in our hearts through a relationship with another person. We have sought the missing pieces of our souls in another imperfect, flawed individual, who generally responds to us from a position of neediness. We have failed to heed God's map and the +directions He has carefully written out for us to follow. He has told us exactly where we can find our wholeness and how our desires can be met:

> [4] *Delight yourself also in the LORD, and He shall give you the desires of your heart.*
> [5] *Commit your way to the LORD, trust also in Him, and He shall bring it to pass.*   (Psalm 37:4–5)

> [33] *But seek first the kingdom of God and His righteousness, and all these things shall be added to you.*   (Matthew 6:33)

For those of you who have been searching for your lifetime mate but have not discovered him or her yet, here is a promise just for you:

> [16] *Search from the book of the LORD, and read: Not one of these shall fail; not one shall lack her mate. For My mouth has commanded it, and His Spirit has gathered them.*   (Isaiah 34:16)

When the Spirit of the Lord draws two people together, you can be assured that the relationship will be "a match made in heaven."

Read on to discover God's starting point on your journey toward fulfilling relationships. As you learn to build and foster the relationships in your life so that they develop into fabulous ones, may God smile upon you in His infinite love and transform your world in His righteousness.

11

It Took a God

G od gave us a fundamental principle for the man-
agement of our lives when He said, *"Let all
things be done decently and in order"* (1 Corinthians 14:40). This general pattern is applicable not only
in the use of His gifts and the conduct of worship serv-
ices, but also in the development of healthy, fulfilling
relationships. Our Lord has also shown us where to begin as we aim for true intimacy with another person. In
order for us to establish a solid foundation on which to
build an unshakable union, we believers generally need
to proceed as follows:

1. Each of us needs to develop an intimate, personal
   relationship with God.

2. Before becoming involved with another person,
   we must first get to know ourselves—who we are
   as individuals and who we are in Christ.

3. If we are to love and accept another person, we
   begin by learning to love and accept ourselves.

The more we grow to love and depend upon the Lord, the more He in turn reveals to us just who we are in Him, and thereby He enables us to love ourselves. And the better we know, love, and appreciate who we are, the better able we are to extend these same feelings and sentiments to our loved ones.

THE SOURCE OF PERSONAL ESTEEM

True self-esteem does not come from our achievements or our material possessions, and it cannot be found in our human relationships. If it could, would people who are financially bankrupt or unemployed or divorced have no value? Of course not! Our real worth is derived from a close, personal relationship with God and who we are in Christ.

As we believers spend time in the presence of the Lord, we allow Him to sanctify us by washing us with the cleansing water of His Word (Ephesians 5:26) and to pour out His love upon us. When the realization hits us that Christ loved us so much that He endured the agonies of crucifixion in order to redeem us from eternal death, we will come to know how truly valuable we are. He bought us with His life! That gives each of us an inestimable value.

Thus, we do not have to find our worth in another person's opinion of us or in how much "stuff" we own or in what we do, even for the Lord. Because our value is rooted and grounded in Christ, we can then enter into relationships with others, not out of our desperate neediness, but out of our desire to share and to enrich our lives.

DEVELOPING RELATIONAL SKILLS

The art of relationships cannot be taught. We must experiment through trial and error in order to develop our own abilities to interrelate. I believe that, to a large

172

extent, we are products of our environments, where most of life's lessons are caught instead of being taught. From the models we are presented, we pick up our views about living, especially about the ways to relate to others.

Such is the case in my life. I grew up in a large family of nine children. Because my father was absent most of the time, our mother was stretched to her limits trying to raise us. She had little or no reserves from which to teach us how to live and love. Survival was the goal in our family. Thus, I found myself looking for love in all the wrong places. I went from one relationship to the next, as each began very quickly but ended just as drastically.

Even after I was born again and had come into the church, that one area of male/female relationships was still distorted for me. Finding myself constantly looking for the right relationship, I invested a lot of time going to the movies and ball games and other events where I thought I could meet the "right" woman for me. Unfortunately, I was involved in a lot of activities that I really did not enjoy, just so I could continue to connect with young ladies who were not compatible with me.

Furthermore, at that time the church had no real training for someone like me in how to live as a godly man or how to act as a gentleman. Since I had come from the streets, I needed to be mentored in how to conduct myself generally and relationally. I had seen my mother being abused and just assumed that this was the way men treated women. Since my dad abused my mother, I erroneously thought that if a man was going to have a good relationship, he had to put the woman "in check" by taking control and exerting authority over her life.

I MET A MAN

Because of my upbringing, by the time I reached the age of seventeen, I was an out-of-control, unsaved young man on my way to prison. Accompanying me into that tiny cell in Rikers Island was my two-hundred-dollar-a-day cocaine habit. There, cornered in that little cell where I could not run and hide, I met Jesus. Later, I would be able to say, along with the woman at the well, *"Come, see a Man who told me all things that I ever did"* (John 4:29). Jesus knew all about me and my past, yet He still loved me and wanted me.

However, it was not until He got me backed up against the wall that I said yes to Him. I thought that saying yes to the Lord was going to get me out of my predicament. Little did I know that saying yes to Him was saying yes to a number of things: yes to His will, yes to His ways, yes to His becoming the Ruler, the Governor, and the Leader of my life.

Surprisingly, I also found that the Man I vaguely remembered hearing about in Sunday school was really a person, a person who could touch me, with arms that could embrace and hold me. His voice would guide and correct me. He blessed me, but He also chastised me.

I discovered the true meaning of love from this Man who provided all the things that I had needed from a natural father but was never able to receive. Needless to say, I was thrilled that there was finally a man, a male role model and father figure all combined into one, in my life. I had tapped into the ultimate relationship. I loved Jesus, and He loved me.

TRANSFORMATION AND DISCIPLINE

Out of this relationship with my Lord and Savior, I began to develop a deep concern for other people. I became compassionate and very sensitive to the needs and hurts of others. I had never really experienced these feelings before. I entered into a discipline through which new qualities and a new character started to form within me. I began to live and act differently from the old me.

In truth, through my relationship with Jesus Christ, I was transformed into a brand-new person. Up to that point, all of the relationships I had been involved in (and had eventually lost) had been a waste of time, because I had not known who I was. When I realized who I was in Christ, I quickly discovered the type of people who would be right for me, based upon the new person I had become through my relationship with Christ.

As I grew closer to my Savior, I learned a number of things about myself and about relationships. First was the fact that there were individuals in life to whom I was very attracted but who were dangerous for me to be associated with. Thus, I had to learn the discipline of distancing myself from people who could be a bad influence on me by not allowing them to get close. Their inticements could have been very detrimental to my walk with the Lord.

Even through the difficult process of relearning how to relate to others God's way, I found companionship in my relationship with Jesus. As He showed me who He was, I in turn opened up myself to Him and admitted who I had been and who I was becoming.

WAITING FOR A SUPERNATURAL INTRODUCTION

Only after I had found out who I was in Christ could I truly embrace another individual and allow her to become an intimate part of my life. It is not until believers find contentment in their fellowship with the Lord that they can truly experience the joys of close human relationships.

However, we need to wait on God to introduce us to His choice of the right mate for us. We tend to want to rush ahead of God's timing, believing that we have become mature enough to handle an intimate union. We often choose a mate hurriedly and therefore unwisely. Because we fail to take the time to know ourselves and to

discipline our lower passions by not permitting these desires to take precedence over our spirits, we find ourselves
in a quagmire of marital confusion and disharmony.

Only God can transform that mismatched, ill-
advised relationship into something of beauty and unity.
But, thank God, He is more than able to take our mistakes, as we surrender them, and to use them for our
good. If He can change us from sinners into saints, He is
quite capable of transforming our bad relationships into
good ones.

> [20] *Now to Him who is able to do exceedingly abun-
dantly above all that we ask or think, according to
the power that works in us.* (Ephesians 3:20)

> [37] *For with God nothing will be impossible.*
(Luke 1:37)

> [28] *And we know that all things work together for
good to those who love God, to those who are the
called according to His purpose.* (Romans 8:28)

THE TRUST FACTOR

When any two people are being knit together in
intimate union, the process often seems a bit overwhelming, yet pleasurable at the same time. When the
two enter into each other's secret closets, they can sometimes exit with the unexpected in shock. However, it is
wise to proceed with caution, because emotions are
highly sensitive as souls are bared by both partners. Not
since the Garden of Eden has it been easy for any of us to
reveal our innermost selves to another person.

> [25] *And they were both naked, the man and his wife,
and were not ashamed.* (Genesis 2:25)

This process of bonding occurs as we risk being
vulnerable with our mates and learn to trust their re-
sponses to our self-disclosures. However, we can easily

violate our spouses and destroy the building trust when we react to their revelations with suspicious accusations. Not only must the couple trust each other, they should most importantly trust God: *"Blessed is that man who makes the LORD his trust"* (Psalm 40:4).

But what does one do when the marital trust has been broken? My marriage had to stand the test of trust, as I was accused of having extramarital tendencies, not with another woman, but with my ministry. Not only was I heavily engrossed in the problems of other individuals, but I mistakenly took for granted the security of my marriage, and I neglected to use proper caution. Although all the material needs of my wife and family were being met, I was failing to meet their emotional needs as well.

GENDER DIFFERENCES IN APPROACH TO LIFE

Men tend to operate from the outside in, while women tend to function from the inside out. Life for men is dealt with from the surface by meeting the everyday material needs of the family and maintaining a certain standard of external structure to the household. However, a woman's creativity comes from within. While the bills must be paid and the home kept in an orderly fashion for a wife to feel secure, all of this must be accompanied by the emotional, mental, and spiritual support of her mate so that she can fully develop her potential. When the husband's promise to be all these things for his wife is broken, her trust in the marriage and her husband is also broken.

So, what do you do when the bond of trust in a relationship has been betrayed and violated? The answer in my case was simply, "It took a God." It took God to use my wife to point out to me my neglect of the marriage, of her and, surprisingly, of God as well. I was so busy doing the work of God that I had gotten out of the will of God.

BINDING UP BROKEN TRUST

While mending what had been torn, I discovered that, in addition to repenting to God, there were also things that I had to do myself. No longer could I attend to others and their problems when mine were not being addressed. First, I had to take the time to reestablish and renew my personal relationship with God. I immediately began to fellowship with Him on a regular basis. Ours was a unique affinity: I ministered unto Him, and He ministered back to me. He placed within me a worship button that He could push at any time He chose. As a result, I entered into a season of weeping, of worship, of divine fellowship with God, in which He became the love of my soul and my life.

I found that as I consistently sought the Lord, the things that were most lacking in me and in my marriage were restored one by one in their fullness. I was reacquainted with my wife and she with me. God's miraculous power of bonding us together in love united us once again as *"one flesh"* (Matthew 19:6) in His sight. This bond is even stronger now than it was then.

MINISTRY IS NO EXCUSE

Some people may argue that as long as a man is doing the work of the Lord, his wife should understand and not complain. However, 1 Timothy 5:8 states, *"But if anyone does not provide for his own, and especially for those of his household, he has denied the faith and is worse than an unbeliever."* In this case, the word *provide* is not to be interpreted as having only a financial connotation, although that is very pertinent. Here, *provide* means supplying the godly support necessary in order to sustain a well-equipped marriage and family, even through the trials and tests of life. Ministers of the Gospel are first responsible for the well-being of their own families.

TRAVELING COMPANIONS

Often a couple must endure hardships together as good soldiers in order to keep the blessing and promises of God within the marriage. This reality is illustrated by the story of Abraham and Sarah in Genesis. Their marriage was ordained by God, who promised to bless them not only individually, but collectively as well. Throughout their many tests and trials, Abraham and Sarah remained faithful to each other. An important factor to remember is that Sarah and Abraham each had a personal relationship with God. Both of them had their faith invested in God and His ability to bring to pass His words to them. At different times Sarah and Abraham had to individually depend on God to meet their needs, instead of looking to one another for the fulfillment of their expectations. Thus, the blessings of God rested on their marriage and even continued down to their offspring. We must understand that although a couple can praise God and pray together, worship, faith, and a divine relationship with God are very personal.

> [9] *Therefore know that the LORD your God, He is God, the faithful God who keeps covenant and mercy for a thousand generations with those who love Him and keep His commandments.*
>
> (Deuteronomy 7:9)

GOD'S PLAN FOR YOUR MARRIAGE

> [11] *"For I know the plans that I have for you," declares the LORD, "plans for welfare and not for calamity to give you a future and a hope."*
>
> (Jeremiah 29:11 NAS)

Discover the plan of God for your own personal life before bringing someone else into it with you. In order to love your mate as God has ordained and purposed in His Word, you must first love God and then love yourself.

²⁸ *So husbands ought to love their own wives as their own bodies; he who loves his wife loves himself.* (Ephesians 5:28)

Marriage is honorable in the sight of God, and both mates should treat this sacred union and their partner with admiration, love, and respect. Putting God first in every endeavor and with each fascinating step in the process of bonding together will help to keep God's blessing on your marriage. "It took a God" for me and my marriage, and surely it will take a God for yours.

12

A Three-Stranded Cord

I f we are to consider ourselves committed Christians, then we cannot justifiably exclude the Lord from any area of our lives. This includes the one area in which we have a strong tendency to exclude Him because it is an exclusive situation—marriage, the most intimate relationship we can have with one other person. However, we must not exclude our Creator from His creation. After all, He designed every one of us with the unique combination of ingredients that make us who we are and that cause others to find us attractive and compatible.

> *⁴ And He answered and said to them, "Have you not read that He who made them at the beginning 'made them male and female,'*
> *⁵ "and said, 'For this reason a man shall leave his father and mother and be joined to his wife, and the two shall become one flesh'?*
> *⁶ "So then, they are no longer two but one flesh. Therefore what God has joined together, let not man separate."* (Matthew 19:4–6)

Were it not for our Creator, then, none of us would stand a chance at the wonderful experience of romance! Our Lord reserves the right, therefore, to be an intimate partner in our personal and marital relationships.

> [23] *For the husband is head of the wife, as also Christ is head of the church; and He is the Savior of the body.*
> [30] *For we are members of His body, of His flesh and of His bones.* (Ephesians 5:23, 30)

God Himself wrote the textbook on love and marriage. First of all, God is the Author of love because it is His essential nature. True love originates in Him and flows from Him to us.

> [16] *And we have known and believed the love that God has for us. God is love, and he who abides in love abides in God, and God in him.* (1 John 4:16)

> [19] *We love, because He first loved us.* (1 John 4:19 NAS)

Secondly, relationships between the sexes and the rules of matrimony are clearly defined and elaborated upon throughout the richly layered text of the greatest book and most delectable romance novel ever written— the Bible. It makes perfect spiritual sense, then, that those of us who are romantically involved and espoused would have as the Head of our relationships the World's Greatest Lover, as well as *"the author and finisher of our faith"* (Hebrews 12:2) and of our earthly alliances.

THE SEASONS OF INTIMATE RELATIONSHIPS

With God holding the reins and directing the individual paths of our lives, He also governs the relationships in which we have become *"one flesh"* with another. His control gives us a great assurance that we are abiding in His will and that our unions are pleasing to Him.

Only with God's guidance will our relationships be certain to last and to be sustained through the cold, rough, inclement winters of romance, even as they flourish and are renewed during the enchanting springtimes.

> [6] *I opened for my beloved, but my beloved had turned away and was gone. My heart leaped up when he spoke. I sought him, but I could not find him; I called him, but he gave me no answer.*
> [8] *I charge you, O daughters of Jerusalem, if you find my beloved, that you tell him I am lovesick!*
> (Song of Solomon 5:6, 8)

These dry seasons of intimate relationships are inevitable. Simply, they come with the territory as we take up permanent residence in the lives of other individuals. The stormy times are part of the process of getting to know others for who they are. As we see them at their best and at their worst, they simultaneously come to know us in the same way. We all need to learn how to weather the worst and delight in the best.

Here on earth, there are no perfect relationships. This does not mean, however, that we have an excuse not to work on our unions tirelessly. Marriage does have the potential to become fabulously fulfilling, if we truly invest the commitment and dedication that we promised to have until the very end, when we first said our vows and became legally joined together.

THE IMPORTANCE OF COMMITMENT

One of the most essential ingredients in a successful marriage is commitment. When we were unattached and dating, ours was the luxury of getting to know different individuals. We could determine what we preferred in a mate and a relationship through our dating experiences. When a relationship hit a dry period, when things were no longer going smoothly or accommodating our preferences, or when we generally lost interest, we could easily dispose of our partners (or be disposed of), essentially because no real commitment existed.

However, in dealing with our mates, the individuals to whom we have vowed lifetime loyalty and fidelity, we must not cast them aside when it seems there is more discord than harmony in the household. This is not an option and should not even be considered. The strength of our commitment when we do not feel loving or loved is perhaps the best measure of the depth of our real love.

We cannot get around the fact that our relationships require our time, patience, humble submission, faith in future possibilities, regular divine intervention, and our resolve to persevere. When we were single, many of us prayed for the perfect mate and relationship, but somehow we expected it to come about without any serious exertion or struggle on our parts. Too many of us, it seems, are simply too apathetic to put in the necessary work a committed, intimate relationship requires.

IT'S WORTH THE EFFORT

At the time of this writing, my wife and I have been married for nearly fourteen years and are most definitely involved in a fabulous relationship with one another. Our marriage, however, has not always been easy. In the beginning, primarily due to the lack of adequate finances to support and sustain our rapidly expanding household—we brought two children into the world within eleven months of each other—my wife and I were at odds with one another. Whether we choose to admit it or not, money often has a lot to do with how smoothly a relationship functions.

At the same time, both of us had neglected our individual connections with God. This was probably more of a contributing factor to the initial difficulties we experienced than even our lack of finances was. Speaking for myself, I was also at a point in my career as an evangelist where I was more involved in the work of God than in His actual will for my life. This served as a major hindrance to the time I spent with my wife. Now that we have both grown considerably in grace and in unity with God's will, we have become much more in tune with each other, and we are both devoted to helping others achieve health and wholeness in their relationships.

I am now able to fully love my wife and support her as she leads a focused, fulfilled, and balanced life. God has taught me to understand her deeply. I see and appreciate the sheer essence of her femininity through simply observing her as she goes about her daily activities, from nurturing our children to keeping our household in order. With all she accomplishes, I am constantly amazed that she is still able to offer me such softly spoken words of comfort and wisdom in my times of distress.

Additionally, we work hard at keeping the lines of communication open. Instead of trying to figure out what pleases each other, we ask. Of course, we do not always see eye to eye on everything even now. Still, we have learned the art of good loving. We understand that it is about giving and taking, about sowing and reaping. We have learned that, ultimately, what you get out of a relationship is directly related to what you have put into it.

[7] *Do not be deceived, God is not mocked; for whatever a man sows, that he will also reap.*
(Galatians 6:7)

DISTINCT MARITAL PERSONALITIES

Although marriage with all of its dynamics does not always live up to our personal ideal, it usually includes many rewards along with the sacrifices. The process of development and growth through conflict and resolution allows each particular marriage to shape and define itself. We must realize that no two marriages are alike. Through conciliation and passionate resolve, the bond of holy matrimony is strengthened and sealed; the lives of two separate individuals become one as instituted in the Word of God:

> [5] *"For this reason a man shall leave his father and mother and be joined to his wife, and the two shall become one flesh."*
> [6] *So then, they are no longer two but one flesh.*
>
> (Matthew 19:5–6)

Therefore, no two marriages should be patterned after each other. God has designed each marriage with its own set of fingerprints and personality, which distinguish it from any other marriage union. Thus, much of the advice we hear about how we ought to operate and function with our partners must be taken selectively. What I share is born out of my own personal experience and is what has worked for me and mine as we have tried to apply godly principles to our particular relationship.

A THIRD-PARTY BOND

Like us, every couple needs the divine guidance of the Holy Spirit in confronting and finding solutions to the problem areas of marriage. Most importantly, we all must seek God for ourselves and apply sound biblical principles to our marriages so that they may be prosperous as well as fulfilling for both partners. *"In all your ways acknowledge Him, and He shall direct your paths"* (Proverbs 3:6). As believers, we need the intimate involvement of that Third Person in our marital relationships if we are to love and abide with one another peacefully and successfully.

However, God is the only Third Party who should ever be allowed in a natural marriage relationship. When He is in the midst, the union is made complete. This means that when coupled individuals first know God for themselves and then proceed to seek the Lord's guidance throughout the development of their relationship, He

186

becomes the glue that binds them together through the good times and the bad, making what was a twofold union become a bonding together of three-in-one. As such, marriage becomes a reflection of the Godhead.

> [9] *Two are better than one, because they have a good reward for their labor.*
> [12] *Though one may be overpowered by another, two can withstand him. And a threefold cord is not quickly broken.* (Ecclesiastes 4:9, 12)

Yes, there is strength in the bond between a couple, but the real source of power lies in the covenant that is formed when Christ is in the center of a relationship.

BY TWOS AND BY THREES

A beautician in my congregation likes to think of a hairstyling process that is most familiar to her, both in her profession and as the mother of four daughters, that vividly illustrates this Scripture concerning the relative strength in numbers. According to her, the braid, which is defined as "three or more strands of hair that are interwoven, interlaced, or entwined together," deftly represents "a threefold cord."

When her daughters were very little, one of the ways she styled their hair was by twisting, which involves taking two bunches of hair, wrapping them around one another, and then knotting them at the end. She says that this was a very pretty way of styling the hair, a style that her daughters preferred, in fact. However, it was also very inconvenient, because the twisted hair would unwind itself, and the hairstyle would come undone in just a few short hours. Twisting, then, became reserved for special occasions, when outward appearance was more important than durability and manageability.

Braiding, on the other hand, was the styling method she applied on a daily basis with her daughters.

Unlike the twisting, which requires two strands of hair, the braiding process calls for three. According to the beautician, this threefold interweaving of the hair sections was a much longer-lasting solution to the problem of tangled, messy hair! Braiding or plaiting the hair may take a much greater initial investment of time and energy than does twisting, but the dividends are well worth all of the work involved.

Furthermore, she notes that once some hair has been styled into a braid, there is no way to tell the three strands apart or to distinguish were one begins and the other ends. It is also impossible to separate or isolate one of the sections of hair from the other two without destroying the entire braid.

Likewise, so it is when we and our significant others have become one with each other and, simultaneously, with our Creator.

UNITED IN LOVE

At the end of His earthly ministry, our Lord prayed this prayer for His disciples then and for us who would follow:

> [20] *I do not pray for these alone, but also for those who will believe in Me through their word;*
> [21] *that they all may be one, as You, Father, are in Me, and I in You; that they also may be one in Us, that the world may believe that You sent Me.*
> [22] *And the glory which You gave Me I have given them, that they may be one just as We are one:*
> [23] *I in them, and You in Me; that they may be made perfect in one, and that the world may know that You have sent Me, and have loved them as You have loved Me.* (John 17:20–23)

May you experience the ecstasy of unity with God and with your special loved ones, and may the Lord restore your relationships to the peak of their fulfillment.